CHRISTMAS

GARLAND FOLKLORE BIBLIOGRAPHIES
(General Editor: Alan Dundes)
Vol. 4

GARLAND REFERENCE LIBRARY
OF THE HUMANITIES
VOL. 343

Volume 4

Garland
Folklore Bibliographies

General Editor

Alan Dundes
University of California, Berkeley

CHRISTMAS
An Annotated Bibliography

Sue Samuelson

GARLAND PUBLISHING, INC. • NEW YORK & LONDON
1982

Library of Congress Cataloging in Publication Data

Samuelson, Sue, 1956-
    Christmas.

    (Garland folklore bibliographies ; v. 4) (Garland
reference library of humanities; v. 343)
    Includes index.
    1. Christmas — Bibliography.   I. Title.   II. Series.
III. Series: Garland reference library of the humanities ;
v. 343.
Z5711.C5S25   1982   016.3942'68282   82-48083
[GT4985]
ISBN 0-8240-9263-5

Printed on acid-free, 250-year-life paper
Manufactured in the United States of America

CONTENTS

Editor's Preface

The Garland Folklore Bibliographies are intended to provide ready access to the folklore scholarship of a particular country or area or to the scholarship devoted to a specific folklore genre or theme. The annotations are designed to be informative and evaluative so that prospective readers may have some idea of the nature and worth of the bibliographical items listed. No bibliography is ever complete and all bibliographies are doomed to become obsolete almost immediately upon publication as new monographs and articles appear. Still, there is no substitute for a comprehensive, intelligently annotated bibliography for anyone desiring to discover what has been written on a topic under investigation.

Christmas is a major festival, celebrated in those areas of the world where Christianity has spread, although it is not always celebrated in religious terms. Its gift-giving component has had enormous commercial ramifications, to the point where the secular aspects of Christmas have threatened to dwarf the religious ones. Christmas has been studied from a bewildering variety of points of view. Anthropologists, educators, folklorists, historians, psychologists, sociologists and theologians have all had their say and as a result it has become increasingly difficult for someone interested in exploring the scholarship to locate some of the critical books and essays.

In *Christmas: An Annotated Bibliography*, folklorist Sue Samuelson has compiled an impressive list of writings on Christmas. From her reading of the materials, she has written a helpful introduction to the subject as well as annotations for the individual items in her bibliography. Users should keep in mind that the materials surveyed tend to emphasize theoretical and analytic treatments of Christmas. This is in contrast to descriptive lists of

Christmas recipes and the like. Scholars and nonscholars alike will find fascinating references in this unique volume.

Sue Samuelson earned her B.A. in Anthropology with distinction in general scholarship and departmental honors at the University of California, Berkeley, in 1977. After a most brief exploratory period in law school, Ms. Samuelson fortunately decided upon a career in folklore. She completed an M.A. in folklore and mythology at UCLA in 1980 and entered the doctoral program in folklore and folklife at the University of Pennsylvania. In addition to carrying out research on Christmas, she has published several essays on American adolescent folklore in professional folklore journals.

Alan Dundes, *Editor*
Garland Folklore Bibliography Series

Acknowledgments

In a work of this sort the compiler owes a great debt to the many individuals whose efforts have been instrumental in suggesting and locating sources. I deeply appreciate the assistance of the following people who helped in translating and/or abstracting various works: Wolfgang Mieder, Donald Ward, Ruth Tennyson, Becky Vorpagel, and Marjorie Dickenson. For providing citations or copies of hard-to-locate articles I thank Bengt af Klintberg, Roger Abrahams, Victoria George, Larry van Horn, Pam Ow, Paul Smith, Linda Dégh, Diane Goldstein, and Eric Wolf. The Veritas Foundation (London), the Hammond Library of the Chicago Theological Seminary, the University of Illinois Library, and the Interlibrary Loan Departments of the University of California, Berkeley and the University of Pennsylvania Libraries were also of great assistance in the location of obscure references. Kenneth Goldstein and Henry Glassie kindly loaned me books from their personal libraries. John Szwed provided helpful comments on the first draft of the introduction. Alan Dundes originally suggested to me the idea of researching the literature on Christmas and has kept a benevolent eye on this project and my development as a folklorist ever since. Most importantly, I am grateful to my parents, Wallace and Catherine Samuelson, for their support and it is to them that this volume is dedicated.

INTRODUCTION

The amount of published material on Christmas and its
constituent customs is immense. Even if one ignores (as much
as is possible) the compendia of Christmas customs or straight-
forward comparative studies and focuses only on the analytical
material, there is still a considerable corpus to survey.
While other holidays and festivals have received scholarly
attention, only Carnival comes close to matching Christmas's
popularity with both lay and academic researchers of calendar
customs.

Why should Christmas invite such enthusiastic study?
Part of the answer is that scholars and analysts are by no
means immune to the "spirit of Christmas" which affects so
much of what they are studying. Some authors, particularly
the earlier ones, have been quite open in professing their
love for Christmas, a love that has inspired them to write
about the season. Recent authors tend to be more cynical.
They believe the popularity of Christmas is due not to any
special magic but rather to the "recurring success of count-
less persons in gratifying desires and in satisfying pressing
emotional needs" at this time of year. Furthermore, "One may
be sure that if Christmas did not make possible the realiza-
tion of individual satisfactions and collective values, some
other holiday would be used to achieve these ends."[1]

But no other holiday has been chosen. Christmas is the
pièce de resistance of the American (if not also the Western)
calendrical celebratory cycle. No one has arrived at an
adequate explanation for this. James Barnett's statement
bemoaning the lack of an "inclusive theory to account for the
origin and development of Christmas" is as true today as it
was when he made it in 1954,[2] although his commendable social-
historical-psychodynamic study and the efforts of many other
people whose works are examined below have gone to considerable
lengths to attempt to produce that theory.

This introduction is intended as a shortcut for readers
who wish to gain a more concise entrée into a particular
approach to the study of Christmas than could be obtained by
laboriously combing the bibliography entry by entry, even with

the help of the subject index to be found at the end of the
volume. Four main approaches to the study of Christmas are
covered: historical, psychological, sociological, and folkloristic. Only key essays or books are mentioned here; other,
less integral works in these areas are referenced in the index
under these same headings. The structure of the four sections
of the introduction varies. Some are organized chronologically
by date of publication to demonstrate the development (or lack
of it) of a research perspective over time. Other sections
fall into place as a result of the various authors' citations
of and rebuttals to each other. (The bibliography itself is
arranged alphabetically by authors' names.) No attempt is
made to discuss strong connections between the categories
since, with the exception of the folklorists, researchers in
one field are largely ignorant of the work done in the others.

Two additional "schools" of Christmas thought could be
proposed: theological and literary. The former is not covered
in any great detail here as it strays rather far from the
parameters of the author's folkloristic emphasis. Nevertheless, some mention of major works concerning the ecclesiastical
history of the holiday is made in the historical section. The
significant studies of Christmas literature and writers' influences on the development of Christmas are few and far between. The best ones can be cited immediately, namely the
last chapter of Tristram Coffin's *The Book of Christmas Folklore*
(1973) and Charles W. Jones's 1954 article, "Knickerbocker Santa
Claus."[3]

In discussing any facet of Christmas--psychological,
sociological, historical, economic, political--the first
source one should consult is James Barnett's excellent book,
The American Christmas: A Study in National Culture (1954).
Barnett emphasizes the division of Christmas customs into the
secular and the religious, but he stresses that there must be
a balance between the two in order to ensure the festival's
survival. Since all Americans, even non-Christians, are caught
up in the activity of the Christmas season, there must be non-
sacred elements for non-Christians to identify with. Barnett
pays close attention to the psychological motivations behind
acts of charity during Christmas--lighter sentences given to
criminals, presents donated to needy children, not to mention
the showering of gifts on one's own children--suggesting that
such charity is in part an overcompensation for guilt at having
given nothing or too little during the rest of the year.

HISTORICAL WORKS

Of twenty major works utilizing the historical approach, only four have appeared since 1950. Most recent works on Christmas have been from either the psychological, sociological, anthropological, or folkloristic points of view; historical studies have appeared as periodical articles rather than book-length works. For this section, then, the best approach to take is, naturally, an historical one.

Three authors, one English and the others German, published Christmas books in the early 1860s; even earlier books exist but they are merely collections of Christmas customs.[4] In his *Weihnachten, Ursprünge, Bräuche, und Aberglauben* (1862), Paulus Cassel concerns himself with several questions that later authors have also addressed: the origins of the Christmas festival, its relationship to other festivals, and folk beliefs of Christmastide. (Other and often overlapping areas of interest to Christmas historians are the Christian adaptations of pagan customs and the relationship between ecclesiastical/ liturgical issues and observances and those of the folk realm.) Cassel maintains that the celebration of Christ's birth was influenced by earlier traditions involving Adam's "birth." He also discusses the Nativity's relationship with Epiphany, and comments on the influence of Egyptian, Greek, Persian, Roman, and Judaic traditions. (See also Usener's *Religion-geschichtliche Untersuchungen: Das Weihnachtsfest* for more information on the effect of customs from the East, Egypt, and Mithraism.) Jewish practices come in for further examination in Section II of Cassel's book, as does the relationship between the functions of Eve and Mary and their relationship to the Christmas story. Section III is concerned with the interplay between folk and ecclesiastical beliefs and customs, especially those involving demons and the devil.

Englishman William Sandys devotes much of his *Christmas-tide: Its History, Festivals and Carols* (1860) to the development of Christmas customs against the backdrop of events in the English court, with a few continental references. General origins are discussed briefly, as are the effects of Puritanism. Sandys then provides detailed historical explanations of specific customs, such as mistletoe, wassail, mumming, greenery, and gift-giving.

The third historical assessment is Johannes Marbach's *Die Heilige Weihnachtszeit* (1865). The author is primarily concerned with pagan attitudes toward nature as they are displayed in winter festivals. Marbach also provides a thorough analysis of the syncretization of pagan and Christian Christmas customs, a discussion that is supplemented by many later

scholars such as Alexander Tille, whose *Yule and Christmas,
Their Place in the Germanic Year* appeared in 1899. While much
of his book focuses on the development of the Germanic concept
of seasonal divisions, Tille does devote three chapters to the
history of the Nativity celebration and the mixing of customs
from various cultures. According to Tille, most winter holiday
customs originated when the Germans adopted the Roman calendar.
For example, the Christmas tree descends from the Roman practice of decorating with greenery at Saturnalia or the Kalends
of January and also from the tenth-century legend of how trees
blossomed and bore fruit at Christ's birth. Tille also provides
a good discussion of the evolution of the Catholic Church's
relationship to secular customs: its banning of them, gradual
acceptance, and then repeated attempts, often unsuccessful, to
control them.

Tille's book was followed in the early 1900s by new works
on Christmas history by William Dawson and Clement Miles. As
with Sandys, Dawson views the development of Christmas customs
against the backdrop of English history in his *Christmas: Its
Origins and Associations* (1902). His chapter titles clearly
indicate the organization: "Christmas, from the Norman Conquest
to Magna Charta," "Christmas, from Magna Charta to the End of
the Wars of the Roses," etc. The preface reveals a profound
sense of Christmas as a part of a process intimately connected
with what occurs throughout the year. "Some of its greater
celebrations marked important epochs in our national history....
The successive celebrations of Christmas during nineteen centuries were important links in the chain of historical Christian
evidences."[5] His approach to a discussion of pagan elements
is also quite perceptive; instead of describing them as having
been swallowed up or mutilated by Christianity, he stresses
their position as links with the past, with older religions,
which were necessary for new Christians in making the transition
from their previous beliefs.

In *Christmas in Ritual and Tradition* (1912), Clement Miles
provides a more substantial approach to the study of Christmas
than the other historians. Apart from Dawson's book, this is
perhaps the best historical work on Christmas. Of special
interest is Miles's relation of the Christmas festival to
general remarks and attitudes on festivity. "It has been an
instinct in nearly all people, savage and civilized, to set
aside certain days for special ceremonial observances, attended
by outward rejoicing," in order to lift people above the common-
place, to escape monotony. The great justification of a feast
was to "wake people up [to] ... sunlit peaks, testifying, above
dark valleys, to the eternal radiance."[6] Primitive feasts
(out of which Christmas partially developed) used a principle

of specialization, of laying up a stock of sanctity--magical, not ethical--for ordinary days. This attitude remained attached to the Christmas festival and is still evident.

Following the general discussion of festivity, Miles claims to want to show the process by which heathen and Christian Christmas elements intermingled, but he proceeds to set off each type from the other. The section labelled "Christian Feast" has chapters on poetry, liturgy, and drama, emphasizing the more serious side of the holiday. The "Pagan Survivals" section is more lighthearted, involving the divisions of the season (St. Clement's to St. Thomas's Day, Christmas Eve and the Twelve Days, etc.) and chapters on the pre-Christian winter festivals, Yule log, tree, decorations, gifts and cards, feasting and food, masking, mumming, and the Feast of Fools. (Further information on specific days, such as St. Barbara's, St. Thomas's, St. Stephen's, and St. John's, can be obtained from Gerhard Müller's *Weihnacht der Deutschen, Aus Geschichte und Brauchtum in der Weihnachtszeit* [1946]. Also of interest is Jacobus Mak's *Het Kerstfest* [1948], the main Dutch work on the history of Christmas.)

The interplay between Christian and pagan was essentially a confrontation, according to Miles, between ascetic principles of self-mortification and world-renunciation and a natural human striving for earthly joy and well being. Try as the Church might to fight heathenism, "mankind's instinctive paganism is insuppressible." Finally, the Church wearied of the fight and thereafter winked at heathen practices. Christmas then became increasingly merry, "suited to the instincts of ordinary humanity." It was "strongly life-affirming; the value and delight of earthly, material things is keenly felt,"[7] yet a certain mysticism remained, a reverence for the meeting of heaven and earth. This attitude is manifested in some of the names for the holiday: "Christmas" implies the wonder of the Incarnation for it is Christ's Mass and emphasizes the liturgical aspects; "Noël" is the birthday and reveals the human side.

Christmas is a microcosm of European religion involving crude magic, speculative mysticism, physical indulgence, and spirituality and tenderness. Miles sums things up beautifully when he writes, "Most men are ready at Christmas to put themselves into an instinctive rather than a rational attitude ... and return in some degree to earlier, less intellectual stages of human development--to become in fact children again."[8]

There was another burst of activity among Christmas historians in the 1930s. D.B. Botte wrote the classic French work, *Les Origines de la Noël et de l'Epiphanie*, in 1932. As a cleric Botte naturally was concerned with the ecclesiastical

history of Christmas. The first chapter of his book covers
the fixing of the dates for Epiphany and Christmas, which re-
lied considerably on Near and Middle Eastern sources of influence. The first Church celebrations of Christmas occurred in
the fourth century and then expanded all over Europe; Botte
looks at manifestations in Italy, Gaul, Spain, the Danube area.
He concludes that Christmas and Epiphany are not just adaptations of earlier Christmas customs from the eastern Mediter-
ranean but basically grew out of early Western celebrations
of the mystery of the Incarnation.

Katherine Richards's book, originally her dissertation,
How Christmas Came to the Sunday-Schools (1934), is another
basic historical work. She discusses pagan elements, the influence of the Reformation, Christmas in the American colonies,
and the appearance, development, and acceptance of Christmas
activities in American Sunday Schools. Her use of political
and social change is much like Dawson's. The period after the
Civil War marked a turning point in American Church celebrations. People became more aware of what they wanted from life,
and the joy and beauty of the holidays appealed to their usual
somber lifestyle, especially after a devastating war.

Another historical dissertation is Leslie Dent Johnson's
"Classical Origins of Christmas Customs" (1937). In it the
author notes the possibility of Nordic pagan influences but
suggests that Graeco-Roman traditions have had the most important effect on present Christmas customs. Saturnalia and the
Kalends of January were the most influential celebrations,
particularly in such areas as the libertine atmosphere (e.g.,
role reversals), food (to secure a bountiful year), mumming,
the Yule log, and greenery.

In *Christmas Traditions* (1932), William Auld emphasizes
the ecclesiastical and pagan divisions of Christmas customs,
which he supplements with chapters on specific customs: cards,
greenery, the Yule log, Christmas tree, gifts, Santa Claus,
and bells. He offers some intriguing comments on Christmas's
position as a festival of childhood and the persistence of
heathen attitudes. Modern people "regard themselves as intel-
lectually 'emancipated' from all pure instinctive attitudes
and primitive modes of thought, which Christianity cannot be
said to have destroyed but only to have sublimated."[9] Primitive
attitudes manifest themselves in a festival commemorating the
birth of a child, which continues to be primarily organized
around children.

Earl Count's *4000 Years of Christmas* (1948) covers
familiar historical ground by noting that the majority of our
Christmas customs developed out of Roman New Year's and

Saturnalia celebrations. More intriguing, however, is his
presentation of the dissemination of seasonal customs from
Mesopotamia. One route was directed through Greece and Rome
where Middle Eastern practices came into contact with early
Christian observances. Another branch came from the Middle
East and meandered through the Danube region's Germanic tribes
before intermingling with Christian ideas. One should note
the contrast between this line of thinking and Tille's attitudes discussed above.

George Buday presents a history of a particular element
of Christmas, the Christmas card (1954). Although Christmas
cards hover on the border between folklore and popular culture,
many of their motifs and greetings are definitely traditional,
as is the custom of their distribution. Buday's work is a good
supplement to the sociological analyses of card-sending (see
below). He notes the presence of traditional Christmas elements:
birds, holly, ivy, scenes of old-fashioned Christmases, children,
and the standard sentiments of peace, love, happiness, but he
offers little interpretation of why these things should be so
popular.

Santa Claus is another element that receives some individual historical treatment, as in Charles Jones's 1954 article
"Knickerbocker Santa Claus." He focuses on Santa's development
in America, particularly the Dutch influence in New York, and
comments on the effect of the writings of Washington Irving
(perhaps as influential in America as Dickens was in England)
and Clement Moore. Adrian de Groöt (see below under Psychological Works) has, however, challenged some of Jones's assumptions and maintains that the English influence of Father
Christmas was more important in the development of Santa Claus
than the Dutch St. Nicholas.

The most impressive of the recent historical works are by
Miles and John Hadfield (1961) and E.O. James (1961). In *The
Twelve Days of Christmas*, the Hadfields follow the usual format
for historical works on Christmas: a chapter on general origins
followed by specific discussions: this time on the symbolism
of greenery, the origins and problems of gift- and card-giving,
the actual identities of the Magi, Epiphany as a pagan survival,
Boxing Day, St. John's Day (December 27), and Childermas
(December 28).

James's work, *Seasonal Feasts and Festivals*, contains discussions of Christmas throughout the book. He takes a litur-
gical/theological rather than a seasonal/peasant point of view,
but is more comparative and developmental than other proponents
of this approach. He stresses how the "rhythm of nature is
reflected in the seasonal sequence,"[10] and wants the reader
to remember how for many centuries subsistence depended on the

vagaries of the environment. Therefore, at critical times of
the year rites were performed which eventually acquired a more
secular character. The turn of the year was one of these
critical points. Supernatural forces were thought to be ram-
pant and the return of the sun had to be ensured. Because the
Nativity was assigned to this date "it was brought into very
intimate association with the mythological victory of light
over darkness and of the rebirth of the sun as the author and
giver of life." Thus,

> at midwinter the coincidence of the Christian Feast of
> the Nativity in its several aspects and manifestations
> with the solar and agricultural customs centered in the
> turn of the year, has brought together in a complex
> and composite pattern the various observances connected
> with both of these significant events.[11]

Several other books on the history of Christmas warrant a
brief mention. Some are basically descriptive works with
brief histories incorporated into the discussions. Alphonse
Chabot's *Noël dans l'histoire* (1910) is an example. It is a
part of an unfinished series of works on "Le Folklore de Noël,
Ou Coutumes populaires de Noël." Another historical approach
focuses on ecclesiastical issues, such as in the anonymous *El
libro de Navidad* (1948) or Wilhelm Hartke's *Über Jahrespunkt
und Feste, Insbesondere das Weihnachtsfest* (1956).

It is difficult to find a truly poor historical work on
Christmas. Those mentioned in the discussion above are the
most thorough or most frequently cited. They are all helpful
in providing an introduction to the general subject of
Christmas and its customs, which is crucial to the attempt to
interpret it.

PSYCHOLOGICAL WORKS

Psychological analyses of Christmas tend to focus on the
darker side of the season. Some authors also freely draw from
anthropological and folkloristic (especially myth-ritual)
theories regarding Christmas. In Ludwig Jekels's 1936 article
"The Psychology of the Festival of Christmas," the author discusses his belief that Jesus' birth marked the crossroads
between old and new. Christ was a replacement for the pagan
sun gods of Rome, Germany, and Scandinavia. Jekels likens
the supplanting of the old by the new to the son's rivalry
with the father. Therefore, Christmas is another manifestation
of the Oedipus complex. The prominence of the Nativity also
is described as an assertion of democratic principles because

it translates the incredible into the understandable by having
the son of God born to a mortal woman. It makes the ordinary
into something super-personal as the result of Jesus' birth.

If Jekels sees Christmas in terms of father-son rivalry,
another psychoanalyst, L. Bryce Boyer, discusses it in terms of
sibling rivalry. In a 1955 essay in the *Journal of the American
Psychoanalytic Association* he states that because Christmas
celebrates the birth of a child so favored that competition
with him is futile, oral conflicts are reawakened and repressed
hostilities toward siblings are released. The oral conflicts
are manifested in Santa's dispensing of presents, which are
symbols for food. The sibling rivalry is represented in the
competition between children for the best presents. It should
be noted that in America Santa Claus is very democratic.
Everybody gets presents; rarely does a child receive a lump
of coal or a bundle of switches for being bad. Even in Europe
these practices are becoming less common. Still, elements of
favoritism are apparent in the distribution of presents, and
even if there is no favoritism, children look for it. Adults
compare gifts as well. People feel guilty because they know
Christmas is supposed to be a time of love, joy, and good will
so they celebrate the festival with a frenzied activity that
leads Boyer to suggest that Christmas may be "a culturally integrated, group manicoid, defensive reaction meant to obviate
guilt related to murder wishes against siblings."

One of the most far-fetched interpretations of Christmas
is presented by Richard Sterba in the *Psychoanalytic Quarterly*
of 1944. He sees symbolic similarities between Christmas and
the unconscious fantasies and unresolved conflicts related
to childbirth. He stresses that it is parental behavior that
reflects this situation. Secret, pre-holiday preparations
are symbolic of conception and pregnancy (for no one can
actually see the unborn child). The last-minute Christmas
rush is labor; Christmas Day is birth with the attendant exhaustion following the opening of the presents. As people
come to view gifts or to bring gifts of their own, they are
really coming to see a baby. Other elements of Christmas receive their due interpretation. Santa Claus is a fusion of
masculine and feminine roles, but Sterba concentrates on the
feminine. Santa Claus has a fat belly, like a pregnant woman,
and his bag full of presents is a doctor's bag, which hides
the instruments important to childbirth. Santa comes down the
chimney, which Sterba equates with the birth canal.

A different approach to the analysis of Santa Claus is
presented in Adrian de Groöt's work *St. Nicholas: A Psychoanalytic Study of His History and Myth* (1965). He focuses on
European manifestations of St. Nicholas, reviewing the mythical

elements surrounding the saint, the history of his Christian
cult, and pagan contributions to it. De Groöt then proceeds
with a Freudian and Jungian analysis, emphasizing St. Nicholas's
roles as the patron saint of *kinderzegen*, everything connected
with children in the biological cycle--maidens, lovers, marriage, conception, unborn children, and birth. The author also
offers an interesting discussion of St. Nicholas as the patron
saint of sailors, stressing the sexual implications of a ship
in port.

In his 1941 article "Negative Reactions to Christmas,"
Jule Eisenbud looks not only at Christmas but also at all
festivals that are observances marked by the individual gratification of infantile wishes normally held in check by guilt.
Some types of behavior, such as the wild sexual activities at
office Christmas parties, are even socially sanctioned. Christmas and the New Year produce the greatest relaxation of the
social superego of any American festival. As a result of the
loosening of social restraint, some people go overboard and
must contend with guilt feelings after normal standards have
returned, or in later years when they remember previous celebrations and cannot enjoy themselves for fear of losing control
again. Some people never can enjoy the holiday season; it is
a time of great depression, sometimes caused by a longing for
past Christmases and the knowledge that present and future
ones can never be as good, and at other times caused by sexual
problems. It should be noted that Eisenbud does not believe
that the pathological reactions to Christmas, even the seasonal-
ly normal ones, are specifically determined by the festival
itself. They are contributed to year-round and are the result
of a long series of incidents.

Perhaps the best psychological analysis of Christmas is
Renzo Sereno's 1951 article, "Some Observations on the Santa
Claus Custom." Sereno believes that children inherently dislike Christmas, and so the motivation for the celebration
must be found in the needs of adults. By creating such a
fuss about Christmas they think they are securing children's
love and ensuring the good conduct they feel is theirs to
exact. They strike a bargain with the children, but this
produces a distance and coldness that robs Christmas of its
altruistic qualities. The idea that a child is under obligation to enjoy Santa is all-pervasive, and if a child were to
be frank about Santa Claus, she or he would arouse in adults
their pathetic insecurity and would expose their quest for
affection. This explains why adults are so keen on insisting
that children be brought up with such beliefs. Each generation
in turn is hoodwinked into celebrating Christmas as it "should
be" and takes out its frustrations on the next.

Another part of Sereno's article examines gift-giving practices among adults. Despite the deemphasis on value--one is never supposed to know how much a gift cost, but can always find out--there is still the essential ingredient of exchange, as can be seen when people talk of exchanging gifts as an activity of mutual obligation. Sereno also brings up the religious aspect of Christmas and notes the lack of religious apparatus in a festival fundamentally sacred. To keep the festival religious would demand personal dedication and maturity and would make Santa Claus unnecessary. Instead, Santa becomes increasingly popular and represents a flight from religion. Few people find the strength to escape from the vicious cycle of the bargaining table to accept the true meaning of Christmas, however much they pay lip service to it.

Very little work has been done in recent years on the psychological problems of Christmas, but a 1967 article in the *Journal of the Oklahoma State Medical Association* by James Proctor examines children's reactions to the holiday. Using clinical data, he analyzes the expressions of anger children display when they discover there is no Santa Claus. Proctor shows that children's expectations of Christmas differ with the degree of psychosexual development they have attained. He believes that Christmas is not always a happy time for children. They are anxious to receive their requested gifts as proof of parental love and their preferred status over siblings. Children are almost always disappointed, because the presents can never be good enough and the underlying instinctual desires represented by the presents can never be fulfilled. This situation causes narcissistic hurt and anger that can range from negligible to severe, depending on the child.

Another relatively recent work is an unpublished dissertation (1968) by Robert Reid. In his attempts to clarify the infantile beginnings of psychological processes, Reid pays particular attention to Santa Claus's being/nonbeing polarity, the holiday's pagan origins, its symbolism of death and rebirth, and especially the coming of light. He believes the celebration of a birth intensifies death anxiety, which leads to general negative feelings at this time of year. Christmas confronts memories from infancy and early childhood which produce the stress, depression, and hostility often encountered in December. Reid then discusses the dynamics of the oral stage of development, which involves trust versus mistrust and the "virtue of hope." This is the critical dimension of Christmas. If the libido is the primary determinant of moods, then the ultimate meaning of Christmas is a crisis between love and aggression.

The last psychological article to be discussed but the
first to have been written is Ernest Jones's "The Significance
of Christmas" (1922). Jones looks at the mythological origins
of Christmas. The season is a time of rebirth; the days begin
to grow longer as the sun reasserts its importance. A new
natural cycle begins at the same time as the birth of the son
of God. The new cycle means an increase in the vital activities
of man, a return to hunting, planting, etc. The eternalness
of the cycle is symbolized in a baby, the baby Jesus, who is
a primordial gift par excellence.

The psychological ideal of Christmas, according to Jones,
is the dissolution of all family discord in a happy reunion.
He believes that historically and psychologically speaking,
the "ultimate significance of all religions and their festivals
is the attempted solution ... of the loves and hates that take
their source in the complicated relations of children and
parents."[13]

Instead of using a psychological approach to explain
Christmas, a group of articles uses Christmas to illustrate
a psychological theory, that of "naturally motivated expectancies." Proctor draws on this idea to some extent in his essay,
but it is best expressed in Craddick's 1961 report, "Size of
Santa Claus Drawings as a Function of Time, Before and After
Christmas," and Roodin et al.'s brief analysis in "Christmas
Tree Drawings Before and After Christmas" (1971). (Both articles cite other, complementary studies.) It was assumed
that children's drawings of Christmas symbols would become
larger as Christmas approached and smaller after the holiday.
The latter was found not to be the case, indicating a residual
effect of Christmas spirit or, as the testers emphasized, a
result of repeated testing.

In addition to reports in academic journals, many lay
psychological articles are found in the December issues of
magazines such as *Psychology Today* or *Ladies Home Journal*.
Examples of these include Benjamin et al.'s 1979 article,
"Santa Now and Then," and Gary R. Collins's "'Tis the Season
to be Jolly'--or Melancholy" (1973). In fact, the lay interpretations have comprised the bulk of the psychological work on
Christmas in the last ten or twenty years. The psychoanalysts,
psychiatrists, and psychologists seem to have abandoned
Christmas in favor of more fruitful subjects. Explanations
for this are almost nonexistent, but it may have something to
do with a researcher's perception of resentment on the part of
others to dissecting a holiday which is held in such high es-
teem; it might be considered sacrilegious or at least in-
sensitive to subject it to intense study. People can more
easily accept a sociological, political, or economic analysis

of their biggest celebration. A psychological interpretation may strike too raw a nerve for many people to handle, much less accept.

SOCIOLOGICAL WORKS

The sociological assessments of the Christmas festival or elements of it date mainly from the 1960s and 1970s. A large subsection concerns the relationship between Jews and Christmas observances, for example, Irving Canter's *Christmas in the Life of a Jewish Teenager* (1960). There are also a few essays on immigrants' adaptations, but these are heavily data-oriented-- what customs were lost or what new ones were accepted--without explaining the social/cultural/religious/economic factors behind such choices.

Two articles deal directly with Santa Claus: John Shlien's "Santa Claus: The Myth in America" (1959) and Warren Hagstrom's "What Is the Meaning of Santa Claus?" (1966). According to Shlien, Santa Claus is a "folkhero" who conforms to Raglan's hero pattern. Santa Claus is symbolic of death and resurrection with his annual recurrence and disappearance; he is also an agent of social cohesion since he remembers all members of a society--young and old, rich and poor (at least nominally),[14] black and white, even non-Christians. (I might add that Santa's appearance in department stores or at office Christmas parties integrates the business world, ostensibly advocating "business before pleasure," with festivity.) Shlien also shows how the Christmas celebration as a whole and Santa Claus in particular work to help children understand moral and religious concepts, and are also a means for elders to "mask their worship of what is ultimately sacred to them, love and responsibility to children who represent the future."[15]

Hagstrom's essay utilizes approaches from several fields in his attempt to understand Santa Claus: anthropology (animism), folklore (solar mythology), and history. His sociological interpretations involve Marxist (Santa as an expression of distress and an opiate of childhood) and Durkheimian (Santa as a sacred figure related to a set of rites) orientations. The changing status and identity of gift-givers in Western society are noted, as well as the reflection of changes in family systems in the roles the gift-givers play. Santa Claus is a complex entity, the repository for many emotions and energies, "simultaneously a father figure, a child control technique and a symbolic representation of affect in small family groups."[16]

Eric Wolf supplements these labels with a designation of Santa Claus as an appropriate collective representation of commodity fetishism. In his 1964 essay, "Santa Claus: Notes on a Collective Representation," Wolf also looks at Santa as a result of the creation of an American culture with a great emphasis on secularism and on relating adults to children. Claude Lévi-Strauss makes a similar observation in two of his articles, "Le Père Noël supplicié" (1952) and "Where Does Father Christmas Come From?" (1963).

Moving from children to a discussion of the family as a whole, Guenther Lueschen et al.'s 1972 analysis of family and ritual in several European countries examines the loss of the identification of Christmas with the Church and Christmas's increasing orientation toward the family. Although the holiday loses some of its functions and meanings, there remains enough interest in the sacred to resist total takeover by modernizing forces. The societies Lueschen studied are moving from more traditional to more modern orientations, but the secularization of Christmas appears as a process of privatization of the sacred, holding onto and intensifying home Christmas customs, rather than a movement of complete desacrilization. Lueschen's work was carried out in four countries (Bulgaria, Finland, Germany, Ireland) and is complemented by three other Eastern European studies by Ribeyrol (Bulgaria, 1973), Nosova (Russia, 1967), and Jelinkova (Czechoslovakia, 1970). One might also want to consult Isambert's *La Fin de l'année. Etude sur les fêtes de Noël et de Nouvel An à Paris* (1976) for a French viewpoint.

Mark Benney et al. also look at Christmas and the family in their report on "Christmas in an Apartment Hotel" (1959). Christmas is seen as a day for reaffirming personal ties, but this attitude is stressed more by women. The mother is central to the Christmas celebration; she stands for continuity. For women in general, Christmas is more arduous but more meaningful than for men. The importance of the family is explored also. Great effort is made by Benney's subjects to spend part of the day with the family, even if ties are not ordinarily maintained. The family is important because it represents security and stability in a social system not noted for these qualities. But again there is a difference between the sexes; women emphasize this family-orientation while men stress their relationship with their friends. Benney claims this difference is due to the training of the sexes, women being more inward-looking and men more focused on extra-familial relationships; however, there are contradictory reports on women's great ability to make friends and maintain relationships.

Three sociological essays on Christmas cards supplement Buday's classic historical work (discussed above). In "The Season's Greetings" (1962), J. Gross explains the Victorian origin of Christmas cards as a result of harsh and rapid social change. Life was colorless and uncertain, so fantasies had to be bright and secure. The more competitive the society, the more need there was for festivals giving the illusion of good will. Sending cards was a way of playing "happy family" by remote control and also a way of keeping in touch with immigrants. These statements and others like them tend to be sweeping generalizations for which Gross provides little supporting material, and they do not take into account the profound class differences of the Victorian era. Nevertheless, Gross's opinions may not be totally inaccurate, and he does make an interesting comparison of the one-time popularity of Dickens scenes on cards with the later appearance of Disney motifs.

Sheila Johnson's brief but excellent articles "Sociology of Christmas Cards" (1971) and "Christmas Card Syndrome" (1971) discuss patterns of reciprocity in the sending and receiving of cards. Her analyses focus on mobility aspirations and economics: the social status of both sender and recipient has more of an impact than religious or ethnic ties. The cards themselves, not surprisingly, reflect the sender's personality, interests, and experiences; particular attention is given to mimeographed letters and cards with political or off-color themes.

Johnson's work has been extended in Kunz and Woolcott's 1976 essay, "Season's Greetings: From My Status to Yours." Their report is highly statistical, but the subject pool was more controlled than Johnson's. The researchers sent cards to total strangers, using three kinds (and qualities) of card to see who would reciprocate and what they would say. Status on the part of the sender as manifested in the quality of the card or return address (from a good part of town) was found to be an extremely important element. Over 20 percent of the recipients responded to these cards and did not even make an inquiry as to the identity of the sender. They assumed they knew the person and it was their fault for forgetting.

The concern with reciprocity is extended to other Christmas activities: gift-giving, parties, exchange of special foods. John Beattie notes how this sense of obligation reflects prestige and power in his article "Tis the Season to Be Jolly-- Why?" (1962). Not only status and economic orientations are reflected but also indebtedness on many levels--personal, familial, emotional, educational--which makes gifts serve a real moral purpose.

Several researchers have noted parallels between the economic aspects of Christmas gift-giving and primitive forms of exchange, for example, J. Davis's article on "Gifts and the U.K. Economy" (1972) or Moschetti's "Christmas Potlatch: A Refinement on the Sociological Interpretation of Gift Exchange" (1979). William Waits's 1978 dissertation, "The Many-Faced Custom: Christmas Gift-Giving in America, 1900-1940," explores gift exchanges as determined by age, social relationship, sex, socioeconomic class, and employment.

The last group of sociological articles to be covered is that concerned with the relationship between Jews and Christmas. Some Jews have adopted various aspects of the Christmas celebration—trees, gift-giving, decorating—which upsets more conservative Jews. Other causes for dismay are school pageants, carol singing, and parties; participation in these events may make Jewish children and their elders uncomfortable. E.G. Hirsch's report (1906) indicates an early awareness of the problem. By the time of Louise Witt's data-gathering in the 1930s the Jew was observing Christmas more than ever. She noted that this participation was of spirit, not theology, and that it could decrease hostility toward Jewish people. She stresses the lure of the Christian majority, but is rather naive and does not mention the counterbalancing efforts on the part of non-Christmas-celebrating Jews to keep others from participating.

The question of Jewish Christmas observances should be examined not only in terms of religious influence but with a consideration of assimilationist factors as well. Milton Matz's 1961 study of second- and third-generation immigrant Reform Jews concludes that a child may need a Christmas tree to "hyphenate the contradiction between his Americanism and his Jewish ethnicism."[17] Here is an example of how performance functions importantly in ethnicity. Second-generation Jews are often against having a tree; they still see it as a religious affront (and undoubtedly a denial of ethnic heritage). The third-generation Jew has secularized the tree and adopts it because it affirms his or her position as an American, although Matz says this kind of person still admires the Jew who does not feel the need for a tree.

A few years after Matz's article appeared, Leonard Gross rejected the ideas contained in it in his own essay, "Jews and Christmas: To Observe or Not? From a New Generation, a New Answer" (1965). Many American Jews of the 1960s began to reassess the assimilationist ways of the parents. According to Gross, the Jew is psychologically free to celebrate Christmas or not, but may embellish Hanukkah instead. (This embellishment may signal that they are not "psychologically free" at all.) In an even later article, "A Jew Looks at Christmas"

(1973), Harold Ticktin notes that no matter what the Jew does
in regard to observing Christmas, she or he still feels "out
of it," for "there is no time of the year that can remotely
compare with Christmas for underlining the continuing apartness
from mainstream America that many Jews feel."[18]

As with the psychological articles, the sociological
essays just discussed approach Christmas and several of its
most important elements from a variety of viewpoints. But
again, there appears to be a lack of awareness of previous
research, especially in the field of psychology, although the
major historical works are dutifully referenced. This fault
is not so common among folklorists, perhaps because of folklore's greater receptivity to using a variety of approaches
in its analyses.

FOLKLORE WORKS

The articles discussed here are somewhat arbitrarily
separated from the other groupings. Inclusion in this category
is based mainly on the authors' status as recognized folklore
or anthropological scholars (e.g., Dundes, Dorson, Abrahams)
or publication in a folklore-oriented journal.

Some of the most distinguished names in anthropology and
folklore have considered Christmas as an object of investigation. Sir James George Frazer could not avoid it in his com-
piling of *The Golden Bough* (1890), but his interpretations are
not surprising in that he emphasizes pagan origins and survivals. He discusses the influence of Mithraic cults, and
like some of the earlier historical writers he devotes considerable attention to the background of the establishment of
the date for observing Christ's birth.

In the 1960s the periodical *New Society* published several
commentaries on Christmas by George Ewart Evans, Claude Lévi-
Strauss, and Lord Raglan. Evans (1966) explained Christmas
as a contest between light and dark, often manifested symbolically in such customs as the Yule log (an assist to the
sun), the hunting of the Wren (fertility), and the Welsh
custom of Mari Lwyd (a person dressed as a horse visits houses
but is not allowed inside because he represents death, yet is
not turned away because that would anger death). Lévi-Strauss
(1963) concentrates on Father Christmas, who symbolizes the
benevolent authority of elders and expresses differences in
status between children and adults. Father Christmas is an
illusion, which when revealed is a rite of passage. Lévi-
Strauss also mentions death, as he perceives autumn to be a
season of the progressive return of the dead. At Christmas

the dead receive presents and disappear until the next year.
An example of this is the Swedish practice of leaving a meal
for the dead on Christmas Eve. Raglan's 1963 article focuses
on the Magi and shows how their story appears in the narratives
of many ancient cultures.

Folklore studies of Christmas in specific societies have
been produced by Roger Abrahams, Alan Dundes, A.L. Shoemaker,
G.E. Nitzsche, David Plath, and J. Stenzel. One of Abrahams's
essays (1972) concentrates on the differences between Christmas
and Carnival celebrations in the Caribbean. Christmas is a
convivial but formal occasion, a time to reaffirm one's place
in the community. It emphasizes group values and involves a
cluster of attitudes regarded as ideal even by the sportier
element of society that later blows off steam during Carnival.

In several other essays Abrahams discusses Christmas mummings. This area has received a great deal of study from
other folklorists, such as Henry Glassie's excellent book,
All Silver and No Brass (1975), or the collection of essays
edited by Herbert Halpert and G.M. Story entitled *Christmas
Mumming in Newfoundland* (1969). Unfortunately, most of the
mumming studies concentrate on historical, comparative, or
structural issues and rarely address mumming's relationship
to Christmas. The same case exists with studies of Christmas
carols, but an exception is Gordon Cox's *Folk Music in a Newfoundland Outport* (1980). He views carolling as a musical
occasion and analyzes the event in functional terms as a
religious vigil and as a social response to the community's
needs, all the while emphasizing its context within the Christmas celebration.

David Plath has produced two articles (1960, 1963) on
Christmas in Japan. To the Japanese, Christmas is a part of
the modern life style, a part of what can make modernity
meaningful. Plath traces the development of the holiday in
Japan from its beginnings in the eighteenth century to its
boom in the 1800s to its present pervasiveness. It is not
perceived as a religious threat by other Japanese religions
since it does not interfere with their own celebrations.
Santa Claus is an important element; he has some connections
with other traditional Japanese figures, is not considered a
moral arbiter, and has been accepted more by the Japanese than
by other non-Western groups which also observe Christmas.

Stenzel (1975) also provides explanations for the Japanese
adoption of Christmas, such as imitation of the Americans
during the occupation and the need for color and gaiety after
World War II. The celebration has been changing with growing
affluence and self-esteem. Higher standards of living have
given it more of a home emphasis. Basically, the Japanese

have taken what they wanted from Christmas--its basic form--
then discarded what was not needed--the deeper substance--and
added their own meanings.

Kaisu Jaakola studies Christmas in a Swedish-speaking
area of Finland in his *Muuttuva Joulu* (*The Changing Christmas*)
(1977). Aside from Ingeborg Weber-Kellermann's work, this is
the only large-scale non-English-language analysis of Christmas
from a folkloristic point of view. Jaakola summarizes his
assessment of the holiday in this way: "Society changes Christmas, although very slowly. Christmas does not attempt to
change society. It attempts to retain what has already been
achieved."[19] Christmas is also a day that can readily be
dedicated, at least in part, to religion as a way of alleviating
the stress that has accumulated from ignoring religion the
rest of the year.

Alan Dundes (1967) has explored Christmas's relationship
to American culture. He stresses Christmas's revelation of
American values and world view. Santa Claus is discussed in
terms of his overshadowing of Jesus, then as a masculine
figure, and then in terms of how belief in him is the result
of parental pressure. Santa Claus is always good to children
because parents dislike administering punishment. Dundes
mentions the uniting of religious and secular social features
through Christmas and that it is a ritual uniting the family
as well. He gives an interesting analysis (derived from
Barnett) of "Rudolph the Red-Nosed Reindeer" as an American
child's success dream come true and examines the commercialization of Christmas, observing that it naturally should reflect
American capitalist motives.

Shoemaker and Nitzsche examine more specific celebrations
of Christmas in America. Shoemaker's 1959 study of Christmas
in Pennsylvania is mainly a descriptive work, but he does
investigate the process of assimilation that many immigrant
customs underwent. The discussion of the development of
Christmas trees and gift-bringers is especially good, but the
analysis of the practice of "barring out the schoolmaster"
makes no reference to similar role reversals that have existed
at least since Roman times. Nitzsche (1941) examines a particular item within a particular group, the Christmas *putz*
(an elaborate *crèche* or Nativity scene) as produced by the
Pennsylvania Germans. His approach, too, is mainly comparative
and descriptive. I have attempted to broaden the approach to
the study of this item of Christmas material culture in
"Nativity Scenes: Description and Analysis" (1979). I look
at Italian, French, and Moravian Nativity scenes from historical, social, and psychological perspectives, stressing how
the Nativity scene can be reinterpreted according to its

context. A similar context-oriented study is Mary MacGregor-
Villareal's essay "Celebrating *Las Posadas* in Los Angeles"
(1980), in which she discusses private and public performances
of the Mexican Nativity play. Richard Dorson has an article
on Christmas gift-bringers in the 1959 volume of an obscure
pharmaceutical journal called *What's New*. He discusses Santa
Claus's differences from other European gift-bringers. Santa
Claus is a caricature of Uncle Sam and embodies the American
love of well being, dreams of abundance, and democracy. He
visits every home and always leaves good things. Dorson also
mentions the European figures, which he classifies according
to their lightness/white qualities or as creatures of darkness,
for example, in Germany, the Christkind as opposed to Knecht
Rupert.

One of the most recent folkloristic/popular culture
studies of a Christmas tradition is Thomas Burns's 1976 examination of a Dr. Seuss book's adaptation to television. "How the
Grinch Stole Christmas" is a popular Christmas television
special and owes its success to the book's fifteen years in
print prior to being adapted to television; the range of
Christmas symbols employed; the variations on the Scrooge
theme; the focus on childhood; and the avoidance of any ex-
plicit reference to Christian religious significance. This
last point is particularly important. The story displays a
wide range of secular Christmas symbols but has only two
religious ones (a star and a dove), and even these are rather
vague. The viewer is free to make any kind of association she
or he chooses, but "the Grinch story suggests that the Christmas celebration may involve Christian religious belief but need
not do so to remain meaningful."[20] Burns's article should
inspire some further scrutiny of the secular/sacred dichotomy
at Christmas.

Many collections of American and European folklore include
comments on Christmas, often with brief historical explanations.
There are also a considerable number of descriptive/historical
articles on specific Christmas customs in folklore journals.
I recommend a perusal of the *Internationale volkskundliche
Bibliographie* or the *Reader's Guide to Periodical Literature*
for those readers interested in such articles. Only within
the last two decades has any concerted effort been made by
folklorists to study festivity in general and Christmas in
particular. Some admirable beginnings have been made but much
material awaits the folklorist's characteristic synthesizing
approach.

CONCLUSION

Overall, what has the study of Christmas produced? By combing the literature discussed in this introduction and in the bibliography proper is it possible to gain a thorough understanding of what the holiday is all about? The answer, unfortunately, is "No." James Barnett has made a good start toward achieving this end, but his work is in need of updating. The excellent historical, psychological, and sociological assessments of the Christmas festival are helpful but far from comprehensive. Folklorists' essays tend to concentrate on specific items or functions, although Thomas Burns's analysis of one element, a Christmastime television program, utilizes the kind of systematic analysis that I think will ultimately be the optimum way of looking at Christmas.

No one has taken a seriously-conceived wide-angle view of Christmas. But again, the question arises, "Is that possible?" Can Christmas as it is celebrated in America, much less its development elsewhere in Christendom, be sufficiently analyzed? Even within the United States the regional, socioeconomic, and historical diversity is overwhelming. An examination of components can no longer be limited even to such relatively "simple" items as trees, Santa Claus, and the like, but involves such complex topics as Christmas in the mass media or the vast economic considerations.

One could try to comprehend Christmas as a whole by focusing on certain aspects that appear to permeate the celebration: public/private, giving/getting, group/individual. I consider the most important of these issues to be the relationship between the sacred and the secular. Despite the laments of those people who want to "put Christ back into Christmas," the festival has never been free of secular elements. It has gone through several cycles of increased sacredness and secularism. Both aspects are important foci for analysis, but even more important is their interrelationship and its effect on the themes and components mentioned above. However, this is just one approach, and it would be unwise to romp through Christmas as it manifests itself in time and space, blithely dissecting every element into its sacred and profane features. Rather than start with the premise that sacred/secular is *the* system in which Christmas functions, one must look at the subject in and of itself to see what it reveals.

Still, the key to understanding Christmas is to accept its vitality as a system, whatever it might be. By taking long hard looks at its history, its customs, and their interpretations by the celebrants one may discover that certain

combinations of symbols, messages, functions, and meanings will
emerge. Such an approach must involve a degree of impartiality
and dedication, but would result in an immensely gratifying
achievement. It would be impossible to take apart every crumb
of Christmas history or every feature of the celebration, but
a thorough analysis of many of its manifestations along the
lines of a modern folkloristic inquiry (utilizing as well
historical, psychological, sociological, anthropological,
economic, theological, and literary approaches) might bring
us to a better understanding of the holiday, which, despite
its changes over the centuries, still is of considerable importance in Western society. Cracking the "code" of Christmas
would also contribute greatly to the comprehension of similar
systems (e.g., religion or festivity in general). Although
Christmas comes but once a year, its influence persists in a
series of complex interrelationships year-round. It is the
researcher's task to figure out how and why Christmas came to
be, and continues to be, such a significant part of the Western
festive tradition.

NOTES

1. James Barnett, *The American Christmas: A Study in
National Culture* (New York: Macmillan, 1954), p. 136.

2. Barnett, p. vii.

3. Works mentioned in the introduction will not be cited
in the notes unless directly quoted. Pertinent bibliographical
data will be found, of course, in the bibliography.

4. See Robert Chambers, *Book of Days: A Miscellany of
Popular Antiquities*, vol. 2 (Philadelphia: J.B. Lippincott
and Co., 1941).

5. William Francis Dawson, *Christmas: Its Origins and
Associations* (London: Elliott Stock, 1902), p. vii.

6. Clement A. Miles, *Christmas in Ritual and Tradition,
Christian and Pagan* (London and Leipzig: T. Fischer Unwin,
1912), p. 17.

7. Miles, pp. 26, 27.

8. Miles, p. 358.

9. William Auld, *Christmas Traditions* (New York: Macmillan,
1932), p. 10.

10. E.O. James, *Seasonal Feasts and Festivals* (New York:
Barnes and Noble, 1961), p. 11.

11. James, pp. 231, 291.

12. L. Bryce Boyer, "Christmas Neurosis," *Journal of the American Psychoanalytic Association*, 3 (1955), 486.

13. Ernest Jones, "The Significance of Christmas" (1922), in his *Essays on Applied Psychoanalysis*, vol. 2 (London: Hogarth Press Ltd., 1951), p. 224.

14. See Billie Davis, "A Migrant Child's Christmas: A Chance to Give and Grow," *New Generation*, 56, no. 3 (1974), 1, 3-4.

15. John Shlien, "Santa Claus: The Myth in America," *Etc., A Review of General Semantics*, 16 (1959), 398.

16. Warren Hagstrom, "What Is the Meaning of Santa Claus?" *American Sociologist*, 2 (1966), 252.

17. Milton Matz, "The Meaning of the Christmas Tree to the American Jew," *Jewish Journal of Sociology*, 3 (1961), 131.

18. Harold Ticktin, "A Jew Looks at Christmas," *US Catholic*, 38 (December, 1973), 25.

19. Kaisu Jaakola, *Muuttuva Joulu: Kansatieteelinen Tutkimus* (*The Changing Christmas: An Ethnological Study*) (Helsinki: Suomen Muinaisamuistoyhdistys, 1977), p. 357.

20. Thomas A. Burns, "Dr. Seuss' *How the Grinch Stole Christmas*: Its Recent Acceptance into the American Popular Christmas Tradition," *New York Folklore*, 2 (1976), 200.

COMPILER'S NOTE

This bibliography emphasizes the study of
Christmas--books, articles, dissertations, and theses
that attempt to analyze Christmas or its customs from
some established point of view are listed. Collections or mere descriptions of Christmas customs are
not included except when supplemented by some significant analysis. In a few cases items are unannotated;
this is generally due to the unavailability of the
items to the compiler.

Anonymous. "Chrissy for the Surfer." *Economist*, 209 (1968), 1332.

This is mainly a descriptive article on the Christmas observances of Australian surfers, but the last paragraph discusses the lack of intensity among sportsmen celebrating the holiday and the contradiction between traditional elements (such as snow and ice) and the Australian summer weather.

Anonymous. "Christmas and Suicide." *Pastoral Psychology*, 4, no. 39 (1953), 7-8, 66.

The author reports on findings that the suicide rate at Christmas is surprisingly low in comparison with the incidence of depression at this time of year. A possible explanation is that the contrast between inner darkness and the length of the days is less dramatic than at other times of the year.

Anonymous. "Christmas Customs and Their Origins." *Nature*, 122 (1928), 964-67.

This article focuses on the origins of several Christmas customs. Mummers plays are an outgrowth of human sacrifice. Christmas itself is an expression of fertility, a feast for the dead, and a reaffirmation of the solidarity of social groups. The differences between Christmas customs in the northern and southern regions of Europe are also discussed.

Anonymous. "The Christmas Tree Legend." *American-German Review*, 15, no. 8 (December, 1948), 8.

This brief article reviews the pre-Christian and Christian history of the Christmas tree and its first use in the United States.

Anonymous. "Christmas without Christ." *Current Literature*, 44, no. 1 (January, 1908), 62-63.

In 1907, the New York City School Board banned sectarian and religious elements from school Christmas celebrations,

especially all songs containing references to Christ. This
article reviews newspaper editorials about the controversy.

Anonymous. "Doggerel in the Manger." *Times Literary Supplement*, no. 3382 (22 December 1966), 1189.

Christmas songs have often appeared on broadsheets.
Their anonymous authors worked within an inherited and
carefully defined tradition. The songs conveyed optimistic
messages of friendship and good will. Some were religious,
some materialistic. Many verses transcended the "deadened
and discredited machinery" to become personal and sardonic.
Contemporary examples are provided.

Anonymous. "Dromedaries and Kings." *Economist*, 213 (1964),
1428.

This is another mainly descriptive article, but it contains some interesting material on changes in Spanish
Christmas customs via the introduction of Northern European
traditions.

Anonymous. "Zur Erkenntnis deutschen Weihnachtessens:
Julzeit—Heilige Zeit." *Germanien*, n.v. (1936), 369-
72, 382-87.

The article examines German Christmas foodways.

Anonymous. "An International Saint." *Nation*, 109 (1919),
789.

A brief history of Santa Claus is presented.

Anonymous. *El libro de Navidad. Las fiestas de Navidad en
la historia, la leyenda, la literatura y las bellas artes.*
Barcelona: Montaner y Simón, 1948.

This is the only substantial Spanish-language study of
the general history and development of Christmas. It places
heavy emphasis on ecclesiastical and literary aspects.

Anonymous. "La Navidad en dos ciudades españolas: Madrid y
Barcelona." *Revista Española de la Opinion Publica*, 31
(1973), 319-427.

This summary of the effect of Christmas on residents of
Madrid and Barcelona reveals that what we believe about
Christmas is true: most people *do* feel happy during the
Christmas season. The holiday has both a religious and
familial character. Information is provided on gift-giving,

vacations, the amount of money spent on food and gifts, and the use of Christmas trees (more popular in Madrid) and Nativity scenes (more popular in Barcelona). The preferred day for giving gifts is Epiphany.

Anonymous. "La Nochebuena en la mesa española." *España Semanal*, no. 220 (26 December 1966), 8.

A survey of the traditional Spanish Christmas foods is provided. They include *porgy*, garlic soup, roast kid, partridge, stuffed chicken, and *turrón*.

Anonymous. "Ritual and Meaning." *Spectator* (London), 213 (1964), 861.

Although Christmas customs are a part of national character, people sometimes want to break away from old traditions. The traditions mean less because of lack of understanding of their beginnings and the little contact modern societies have with traditional religion. Christmas balances Easter, through the crowded stable versus the empty grave, life versus death.

Anonymous. "Turning on Christmas: History of Electric Christmas-Tree Lights." *Newsweek*, 74, no. 26 (29 December 1969), 8.

The article is true to its title's promise.

Anonymous. "Vision of Reality." *Spectator* (London), 209 (1962), 952.

The anonymous author advocates a less manic celebration of Christmas. One should have fun but not become ill or unhappy. He thinks he sees this counterrevolution actually occurring.

Anonymous. "Wien und der Weihnachtskrippenbau in Bohem und Mahren." *Zeitschrift für Ostforschung*, 22 (1973), 515-27.

This history of Bohemian and Moravian Nativity scenes from the Reformation to 1945 includes information on their functions as instruments of indoctrination, works of art and folk art, and articles of commerce.

Abrahams, Roger D. "Christmas and Carnival on St. Vincent." *Western Folklore*, 31 (1972), 275-89.

Abrahams discusses the obvious and not-so-obvious differences in the celebrations of Christmas and Carnival on

a Caribbean island. He provides a sociological interpretation of Christmas as a convivial but formal occasion and a
time to reaffirm one's place in the community because of
the holiday's emphasis on group values. Christmas involves
a cluster of attitudes regarded as ideal even by the sportier
elements of society who later blow off steam during Carnival.

————. "Christmas Mummings on Nevis." *North Carolina Folklore*, 21 (1973), 120–31.

This mainly descriptive article does provide some comparative material on mumming.

————. "The Cowboy in the British West Indies." *Publications of the Texas Folklore Society*, 32 (1964), 168–75.

This description of a Christmas folk play/mumming points
out elements derived from English mummings and from American
culture, such as the use of cowboy-and-Indian characters.

————. "'Pull Out Your Purse and Pay': A St. George Mumming
from the British West Indies." *Folk-Lore*, 79 (1968),
176–201.

Abrahams mentions the relationship between the season of
mumming performances and their dramatic structure but does
not develop the idea. The emphasis is on the development
of specific characters and dialogue.

Agurskij, M.S. "Die Judenchristen in der Russische-Orthodoxen
Kirche." *Ostkirchliche Studien*, 23 (1974), 137–76 and
281–300.

Alemany Vich, Luis. *Pequeña historia de la felicitacion
navidena*. Monografias de arte, vid, literatura y paisaje,
19. Palma and Mallorca: Panorama Balear, 1952.

The author provides an historical study of Christmas
greetings—poems, postcards, greeting cards, important
words.

Alexe, Gheorghe. "Legătura êntre om şi firea êneonjură toare
ên cokundele romîneşti" ("The Relationship between Man
and the Outside World during Romanian Christmas Celebrations"). *Mitrapolia Olteniei*, 8 (1956), 200–209.

Alvarez Solar-Quintes, Nicolás. "Villancicos tradicionales
de Asturias." *Boletín de Instituto de Estudios Asturianos*,
20, no. 59 (1966), 79–88.

This examination of traditional Asturian Christmas songs also mentions the replacement of older traditions by trees and electric lights.

Amades, Joan. *El pessebre*. Barcelona: Aedos, 1959.

Amades provides an extensive examination of Nativity scenes: their history (including archaeological records and Gothic, Renaissance, Baroque, and Romantic examples), geographical distribution, the development of various terms (*pessebre*, *crèche*, etc.), associated activities (plays, beliefs, music, dance), and the figures and their construction. The volume contains an extensive bibliography.

Andersson, Eric H. "Jul och julfirande i gangna tider." *Folkkultur*, 5 (1945), 140–59.

Appia, G. *Noël à travers les âges*. Genève: n.p., 1914.

Auld, William Muir. *Christmas Traditions*. New York: Macmillan, 1932; rpt. Detroit: Gale, 1968.

Auld discusses the fixing of the date of Christ's birth and the development of pagan contributions to Christian Christmas observances. He provides excellent material on Christmas carols and believes the singing of Christmas songs grew out of the Nativity scene (*crèche*) observance. This is one of the basic historical works.

Babb, Harold Kenneth. "A Christmas Play as a Model for Telling the Christian Story through Chancel Drama." Diss. Drew University, 1979.

Members of a congregation write and produce a Christmas play to capture the wonder and glory of the Nativity in a contemporary setting. This activity interweaves the human story with the biblical one. A history of religious drama is also provided.

Baker, Margaret. *Discovering Christmas Customs: A Discovering and Folkloric Guide to Seasonal Rites*. Tring, England: Shire, 1968; 2nd edition, 1972.

Some historical material is presented in this small, popular book on Christmas customs, ceremonies, beliefs, games, and cards.

Barnett, James H. *The American Christmas: A Study in National Culture*. New York: Macmillan, 1954.

Although somewhat dated, this remains the best book on
Christmas as it combines historical, sociological, and
psychological interpretations. Barnett discusses the contributions of immigrant groups, the humanistic influence of
Dickens, the social role of Santa Claus (with a brief
psychological interpretation). He also looks at the importance of women and the family in Christmas celebrations
and the holiday's effect on community integration, such as
the relationships reflected in gift-giving. The song and
story of Rudolph the Red-Nosed Reindeer provides the im-
petus for a fascinating analysis.

————. "Christmas in American Culture." *Psychiatry*, 9
     (1946), 51-65.

Barnett states that the significance of Christmas to
individuals varies widely and accords with childhood training. He traces the historical development of religious
and secular elements in the United States and discusses
the pattern of gift exchange as a representation of status
relations, including age and sex factors. This excellent
article also examines important factors contributing to
Christmas's popularity, such as the emphasis on strengthening
family unity and giving adults a chance to become children
again.

Battle, M. "Seasonable Gloom." *Spectator* (London), 209
     (1962), 890-91.

Battle's essay is a lay psychological and sociological
analysis. He discusses the relationship between children
and Santa. Children are happy at Christmas, but then reflect upon their status as sinners and become unhappy with
themselves, feeling unworthy and depressed. They also feel
ambivalence because of sibling rivalry. Elders experience
Christmas as a season of anxiety; they are tired but feel
it is their duty to put on a front and conceal problems.

Baur, John E. *Christmas on the American Frontier: 1800-1900*.
     Caldwell, Idaho: Caxton, 1961.

Even if the pioneers celebrated no other occasion, they
remembered Christmas. Observances were sometimes rowdy,
but their spiritual nature always showed through. The impact of immigrant groups changed American Christmas celebrations early on. This historical and descriptive work pays
special attention to Christmas in California, Texas, the
Rockies, the Pacific Northwest, and Alaska among explorers,
fur men, gold miners, Mormons, Indians, soldiers, and cowboys.

Beattie, John. "Tis the Season to Be Jolly--Why?" *New Society*,
1, no. 13 (27 December 1962), 12-13.

Beattie maintains that Christmas activities are not performed simply out of good will; one expects reciprocity.
There is a sense of obligation involved in gift exchange
that reflects prestige and power as well as "moral" motivations.

Becker, Albert. "Urkundliches zur Geschichte des Weihnachtsfestes." *Hessisches Blätter für Volkskunde*, 32 (1933),
158-64.

Becker traces the tradition of the Christmas tree back
to religious paradise plays and points out that the Christmas
tree moved from the Church into the home around 1600. He
also discusses the tradition of giving gifts on St. Nicholas's
Day, which was later adopted for Christmas as well. In the
seventeenth century, the Christmas tree and Christmas gifts
became more accepted in Germany; Becker demonstrates this
with quotations from literary texts of that time.

Belfrage, Sixten. "Till julklappssedens historia." *Folk-
minnen och Folktankar*, 22 (1935), 75-87.

Belfrage presents a selective history of Christmas
celebrations in Scandinavia in the eighteenth and nineteenth centuries.

Bencker, Georg. "Das deutsche Weihnachtsspiel." Diss.
Ernst-Moritz Arndt-Universität, 1933. Berlin: Adolf
Gerhardt, n.d.

Bencker presents a thorough historical study of Christmas
plays, folk and liturgical. The various kinds of drama--
Magi play, Herod play, star singers--are discussed, as are
medieval, sixteenth- and seventeenth-century, and contemporary (Bohemian, Hungarian, Bavarian) versions.

Benjamin, Ludy T., Jr.; Jacqueline F. Langley; and Rosalie J.
Hall. "Santa Now and Then." *Psychology Today*, 13,
no. 7 (December, 1979), 36-44.

The authors compare the answers of children on two
questionnaires, one from 1896 and one from 1977, adminis-
tered in Lincoln, Nebraska. The children in the 1977 study
were less likely to consider Santa Claus as superhuman,
were older when they first learned his true identity, received the news from parents rather than peers, and were
not disillusioned with Santa Claus and wanted to pass on

the belief to their children. Some general comments are
made on the role of fantasy in child development.

Benney, Mark, et al. "Christmas in an Apartment Hotel."
    American Journal of Sociology, 65 (1959), 233-40.

    Benney's research has produced an excellent article.
    Apartment-hotel residents were used to study Christmas
    images and activities. Christmas is seen as a day for
    reaffirming personal ties, but this is stressed more by
    women. Women also stress the family and past Christmases;
    men stress their friends. The mother is central to the
    celebration of Christmas as she represents continuity.
    Great effort is made to spend part of the holiday with the
    family even if ties are not maintained ordinarily. The
    family is important at this time because it represents
    security and stability in a social system not noted for
    these qualities.

Berglund, Barbro. "Jultomtems ursprung." *ARV*, 13 (1957),
    159-72.

    Jultomtem is the Swedish equivalent of Santa Claus. The
    author discusses the influence of foreign gift-giving
    characters, models within Swedish folklore, and the influ-
    ence of the Swedish media, especially the work of artist
    Jenny Nyström.

Berne, Eric. "Games People Play at Christmas." *Transactional
    Analysis Journal*, 8 (1978), 322-35.

    Although laden with transactional analysis jargon,
    Berne's article contains some interesting comments on the
    socially and psychologically destructive aspects of
    Christmas activities. He feels the essence of Christmas
    is communion--with religion, nature, family, and personal
    remembrances.

Bettelheim, Judith. "The Afro-Jamaican Jonkonnu Festival:
    Playing the Forces and Operating the Cloth." 2 vols.
    Diss. Yale University, 1979.

    This study of a secular Christmas festival covers origins
    and development, structure, choreography, characters, cos-
    tume, and masking, emphasizing the interweaving of theatrical
    traditions from Africa and Britain.

Bishop, Eric F.F. "Bethlehem and the Nativity: Some Traves-
    ties of Christmas." *Anglican Theological Review*, 46
    (1964), 401-13.

Many aspects of the Christmas story are Western apocryphal creations, not gospel, including the concepts of the stable, poor, rough shepherds, a ragged Holy Family, straw or hay in the manger, and the date of Christ's birth as December 25.

Blanshard, Paul. *Religion and the Schools: The Great Controversy.* Boston: Beacon, 1963.

Blanshard makes a few comments on the legal conflicts concerning the celebration of Christmas in public schools.

Blenkinsopp, Joseph. "Why Keep On Celebrating Christmas." *Commonweal*, 95 (1971), 302-3.

The author reviews the myths and legends surrounding the primary Christmas story and symbols. He also provides a critique of the role of Santa Claus in American Christmas celebrations.

Bø, Olav. *Var Norske Jul.* Oslo: Det Norske Samlaget, 1974.

This historical/descriptive work is ordered chronologically, covering the customs of pre-Christmas, Christmas Eve, Christmas Day, the day after Christmas, and New Year's.

Bosch, Karl. "Weihnachten in der Provence. Eine volkskundlich-soziologische Studie zum Wesen von Kultformen." *Oberdeutsche Zeitschrift für Volkskunde*, 4 (1930), 1-22.

Bossard, James H.S., and Eleanor S. Boll. *Ritual in Family Living: A Comparative Study.* Philadelphia: University of Pennsylvania Press, 1950.

This excellent but rarely cited survey of ritual, holidays, and celebrations within family settings includes some mention of Christmas customs, usually accompanied by a brief sociological analysis.

Bot, Nicolae. "Contribuţii la cunoşterea funcţiei colundelor" ("Contributions to the Understanding of the Function of Christmas"). *Anuarul Muzeului Etnografic al Transilvaniei* (1971-1973), 473-88.

Botte, D. Bernard. *Les Origines de la Noël et de l'Epiphanie, étude historique.* Abbaye du Mont César, Louvain: n.p., 1932.

One of the classic French works on Christmas, Botte's study emphasizes theological material. His concerns include the establishment of the date of Christmas and of Epiphany

in the Near and Middle East, then the holiday's first ap-
pearances in Europe around the early fourth century and its
subsequent development. Specifics on the various observances
in .Italy, Gaul, Spain, and the Danube are provided. Botte
concludes that Christmas and Epiphany were not just Western
adaptations of early Eastern Christian customs; there was
considerable exchange between Eastern and Western theologies,
and both holidays grew out of the diverse early celebrations
of the mystery of the Incarnation.

Boyer, L. Bryce. "Christmas Neurosis." *Journal of the American
    Psychoanalytic Association*, 3 (1955), 467-88.

    Christmas rekindles earlier memories of anal frustration
and sibling rivalry. One is competing with the Christchild,
a sibling so favored that competition is futile. Santa
Claus and gift-giving are focal points for oral conflicts.
Boyer asks, "Is the celebration of Christmas a culturally
integrated, group manicoid, defensive reaction meant
to obviate guilt related to murder wishes against siblings?"

Bricker, Victoria Reifler. *Ritual Humor in Highland Chiapas*.
    Austin: University of Texas Press, 1973.

    Bricker discusses customs occurring during Christmas and
Epiphany, a prime festival period and occasion for ritual
humor.

Brooks, A.T. "Origin of Christmas Carols." *Arts and Decora-
    tion*, 12 (1919), 103.

    Brooks gives a brief, general history of Christmas carols
and includes some comments on the effects of the Puritan
repression of Christmas celebrations.

Brown, Abraham English. "The Ups and Downs of Christmas in
    New England." *New England Magazine* (Boston), n.s., 29
    (1903), 479-84.

    Brown details the history of Christmas celebrations in
New England, with particular reference to Puritan influences.

Brummer, Fred. "The Mummers." *Beaver: Magazine of the North*,
    56 (Winter, 1966), 24-25.

    This short history and compilation includes examples of
mumming activities from French Canada.

Bryant, A. "Juxtaposition of Earth and Heaven in Christ's
Birth at the Root of Every Christmas." *Illustrated London News*, 241 (1962), 1002.

Despite its impressive title, this is a typical "What Is
Christmas?" article. It does offer some lay psychological
interpretation, pointing out that Christmas is a time when
the world forgets that it is the world with all of its evil
and harmful elements. People know how things are but take
the time to honor the good and celebrate the possibility
of hope.

Buday, George. *The History of the Christmas Card*. London:
Rockliff, 1954; rpt. Detroit: Gale, 1971.

This book is a thorough survey of Christmas cards and
their development since the mid-nineteenth century and
their various motifs, scenes, and greetings.

Bülow, Paul. "Unser Weihnachtsbrauchtum im Spielgelbild der
deutschen Dichtung. Ein Beitrag zur deutschkundlichen
Unterreichtspraxis." *Zeitschrift für Deutschkunde*, 43
(n.d.), 806-13.

Bülow's pedagogical essay is concerned with how one could
teach the customs of Christmas in the schools of Germany.
He discusses Christmas customs in a number of nineteenth-
century German literary works, including prose works by
Wilhelm Raabe, Peter Rosegger, E.T.A. Hoffmann, and Fritz
Reuter. Bülow also deals with Thomas Mann's depiction of
Christmas in his novel *Buddenbrooks*.

Burckhardt-Seebass, Christine. "Freiheitsbaum und Weihnachtsbaum. Eine historische Miniatur." *Schweizerisches Archiv
für Volkskunde*, 73 (1977), 127-37.

The author investigates the historical and folk-religious
relationships between the Christmas tree and the Maypole.

Burland, C.A. *Echoes of Magic: A Study of Seasonal Festivals
Through the Ages*. London: Peter Davies, 1972.

Burland comments on ancient winter festivals and the
development of the Christmas season, including a discussion
of the various days that could be considered the official
start of the season: Thanksgiving, St. Clement's Day, St.
Catharine's Day. Santa Claus is analyzed in terms of
sexual content and also related to Pueblo Kachina practices.
Burland feels that Christmas has not been overly commer-
cialized but has acquired more glamour over the years.

Burns, Thomas A. "Dr. Seuss' *How the Grinch Stole Christmas*:
    Its Recent Acceptance into the American Popular Christmas
    Tradition." *New York Folklore*, 2 (1976), 191-204.

    Burns explores the reasons for the Grinch story's popu-
    larity in print and on television. It uses an array of
    standard Christmas symbols (gifts, food), but excludes any
    references directly pertaining to Christian religion. Such
    associations can be made by the viewer because the main
    themes are in harmony with religious aspects of Christmas
    but are not directly employed. "Boiled down to its didactic
    essence, the Grinch story suggests that the Christmas
    celebration may involve Christian religious belief but
    need not do so to remain meaningful" (p. 200). The program's
    continuing popularity as a seasonal television favorite is
    also explored and is attributed to the book's fifteen
    years in print prior to its adaptation for television, the
    range and type of Christmas symbols used, the variations on
    the Scrooge theme, the focus on childhood, and the avoidance
    of explicit religious references.

Čajkanović, Veselin. "Nekolike primedbe uz srpski Badnji dan
    i Božić." *Godišnjica Nikolde Cupića* (Belgrade), 34
    (1921), 258-80.

    This article explores the correspondences between Chris-
    tian Serbian Christmas celebrations and pagan Serbian
    totemic feasts.

Ćalić, Alija. "Božić kod Musliman" ("Christmas Among the
    Muslims"). *Zbornik za Narodni Život*, 26 (1928), 379.

Campbell, R.J. *The Story of Christmas*. New York: Macmillan,
    1934.

    A wide-ranging historical/descriptive work, Campbell's
    book begins with a discussion of the fixing of the date of
    Christ's birth, then moves to a presentation of stories
    associated with the birth (e.g., animals talking). Tribu-
    tary festivals such as the North European Yule, the Roman
    Saturnalia, and Mithraic observances are mentioned along
    with work on non-Christian customs. Later English customs
    which interest Campbell include the use of the Christmas
    tree, a Santa Claus-type figure, stories, carols, verse,
    plays, and the development of an emphasis on children
    during the holiday season.

Campbell, Thomas P. "The Liturgical Shepherds Play and the
    Origins of Christmas Drama." *Mosaic*, 12, no. 2 (Winter,
    1979), 21-32.

Campbell questions the traditional chronology of the development of medieval shepherds plays as parts of Christmas drama.

Canter, Irving. *Christmas in the Life of a Jewish Teenager: A Study of the Attitudes of Members of B'nai B'rith Youth Organization toward Holiday Observances in the Public School--December, 1960.* New York: Anti-Defamation League of B'nai B'rith, 1960.

This is a short (19 pp.) summary of a 1960 survey of Jewish teenagers' attitudes toward Christmas. Informants were polled on the types of Christmas and Hanukkah activities in their schools and their feelings about the frequency of Hanukkah activities. The questions of isolation, hostility, intergroup relations, and assimilation were also explored. The results reveal few objections to Christmas activities in school, especially if religious elements are eliminated. Some subjects were disturbed by having to sing religious Christmas songs. There was an acknowledgment of the lack of carry-over of Christian activities into daily life, although some secular symbols (trees, wreaths, stockings, cards, Santa Claus, candy canes, lights) did appear. Canter concludes that the favorable attitudes of administrators to Christmas observances in the public schools are not likely to change and that Jewish educators should explore further the meanings of Hanukkah and Christmas.

————. "Uncle Sam, the Hanukkah Man: Assimilation or Contra-Culturation?" *Reconstructionist*, 27, no. 9 (December, 1961), 5-13.

The Christmas-Hanukkah problem is largely perceived as a problem of assimilation or deculturation. Canter feels that this argument is silly; the use of Hanukkah bushes or Uncle Sam the Hanukkah Man is an example of selective borrowing and countervalues, just as Hanukkah candles were an adaptation of a Hellenistic pattern for celebrating a victory. Canter explores the applications to the controversy of such concepts as syncretism, reinterpretation, and role ambiguity.

Caplow, Theodore, and Margaret Holmes Williamson. "Decoding Middletown's Easter Bunny: A Study in American Iconography." *Semiotica*, 32 (1980), 221-32.

The main thrust of this article is an examination of the Easter Bunny as a symbol in an American community. The

Easter Bunny is compared to Santa Claus and, on a larger
scale, Easter and Christmas are contrasted. Both holidays
consist of a culminating day surrounded by a season with
subsidiary celebrations. A vacation is granted to workers
and students; gifts and cards are exchanged; families are
reunited, most dramatically at a major meal. The authors
note a vast amount of redundancy in the various activities
which stress their importance to the community. The social-
symbolic aspects of gift exchanges are mentioned, especially
with regard to the emphasis on children. The indoor settings of the Christmas season are also explored, as are the
connections between secular and religious symbols. Christmas is summed up as a festival in which social relationships
are emphasized and clarified (especially the dependency
of children), in contrast to the blurring of social relationships at Easter.

Carneiro, Edison. "As pastôras de Natal." In *25 estudios
de folklore. Homenaje a Vicente T. Mendoza y Virginia
Rodriguez Rivera*. Mexico City: Universidad Nacional
Autónoma de Mexico, Instituto de Investigaciones Estéti-
cas, 1971, pp. 249-57.

Carneiro discusses three types of Spanish shepherds
plays: the *pastorinhas*, *presepios*, and *bailes pastoris*.
He believes that they derive from a semi-learned rather
than pure folk tradition.

Cassel, Paulus. *Weihnachten, Ursprünge, Bräuche, und Aberglauben*. Berlin: Ludwig Raub, 1862; rpt. Walluf bei
Wiesbaden: Martin Sändig, 1973.

Cassel's book is one of the major German works on Christmas. He begins with the origins of the Christmas festival,
which was influenced by earlier traditions concerning
Adam's birth and celebrations on January 6, Epiphany, as
well as by Persian and Mithraic festivals. He then discusses the names and customs of related festivals such as
Hanukkah, the development of the word "Weihnacht," elements
such as Christmas trees, manger scenes, and signs of nature.
Cassel then moves into an extensive description and history
of folk beliefs surrounding the Christmas season.

Catell, James P. "The Holiday Syndrome." *Psychoanalytic
Review*, 42 (1955), 39-43.

Catell notes that the part of the year from Thanksgiving
to New Year's is a time of depression and anxiety for some
people. They feel helplessness, nostalgia, and irritability,

along with a desire to magically resolve problems. These
feelings are at their peak at Christmas.

Celander, Hilding. *Förkristen jul, enligt norröna kallor.*
Göteborgs Universitets Årsskrift, vol. 61, no. 3. Stockholm: Almqvist and Wiksell, 1955.

This basic study of the Scandinavian pre-Christian Yule
covers the effects of old Norse customs, festivals, religion,
and narratives on later Christmas celebrations.

————. *Nordisk jul*, vol. 1. Stockholm: H. Gebers, 1928.

Although this was planned as a two-volume work, only the
first volume was published. The author thoroughly surveys
(à la Mannhardt) the old peasant customs related to Christmas in Nordic countries.

Cesaresco, E.M. "Origin of Christmas Celebrations and Plays."
Contemporary Review, 77 (1900), 117-23.

Cesaresco provides an historical discussion of the portrayal of Christ's Nativity in art, song, and drama.

Chabot, Alphonse. *Noël dans l'histoire; Ou Ephémérides de
Noël.* Pithiviers: Impr. Moderne, 1910.

Chabot produces vignettes involving Christmas celebrations at various points in time and space. No analysis or
discussion is provided, but Chabot's work is significant
because he planned to write a series of works on "Le Folklore de Noël, Ou Coutumes populaires de Noël." The series
was not completed, but among the titles published, by the
same publisher, are: *Les Crèches de Noël dans tous les
pays* (1906); *La Fête des rois dans tous les pays* (1908);
Noël dans les pays étrangers (1906); and *La Nuit de Noël
dans les pays étrangers* (1907).

Chambers, E.K. *The English Folk-Play.* Oxford: Clarendon,
1933; rpt. New York: Russell and Russell, 1964.

Chambers explores the texts, variants, and history of
various seasonal plays. No real applications to Christmas
are portrayed.

Chambers, Robert, ed. *Book of Days: A Miscellany of Popular
Antiquities*, vol. 2. Philadelphia: J.B. Lippincott Co.,
1914.

Arranged chronologically according to days of the year,
this work is a collection of anecdotes, stories, and verse

but contains some historical material on Christmas (pp. 733-67) and St. Nicholas (pp. 661-66).

Chase, Ernest Dudley. *The Romance of Greeting Cards*. Cambridge, Mass.: University Press for E.D. Chase, 1926; rpt. Dedham, Mass.: Rust Craft Publishers, 1956.

The book contains a section on the history of Christmas cards.

Chaves, Luís. *O Natal em Portugal*. Lisbon: Campanha nacional de educação de adultos, 1955.

Chesterton, G.K. "On Christmas That Is Coming," in his *Avowals and Denials*. London: Methuen, 1934, pp. 7-12.

Because of continual promotion, Christmas has become something to anticipate rather than to enjoy. There is more fuss about the approach of Christmas than concern for making Christmas itself really festive. This results from our orientation toward future, rather than present, happiness.

————. "The Spirit of Christmas," in his *The Thing: Why I Am a Catholic*. New York: Dodd, Mead, 1930, pp. 249-55.

Christmas is a feast dedicated to domesticity, but it takes place mainly outside the home in shops, streets, and on line. What is called the spirit of Christmas is still too focused on externals. Chesterton desires a much more home-oriented, self-contained observance.

————. "The Yule Log and the Democrat," in his *The Uses of Diversity*. London: Methuen, 1920, pp. 138-43.

If Christmas is a *time*, the Yule log and other fire-associated Christmas customs (lights, candles) provide a *place* or *frame* for experiencing Christmas.

Church, Francis Pharcellus. "Editorial: Yes, Virginia...." *New York Sun* (21 September 1897).

Although Church's name is unfamiliar to most people, his famous editorial is known worldwide. He was a sometimes skeptical editorial writer on religious topics who on this occasion chose to stress the philosophy of hope and love. The editorial is reprinted in many popular books. For a reprint and summary of its history see E. Willis Jones, *The Santa Claus Book* (New York: Walker, 1976), pp. 124-25.

Clemente, Thomas A. "Double or Nothing." *Commonweal*, 53 (1950), 273–74.

This insightful article on Christmas and Hanukkah observances in public schools objects to the attempt to keep
religion out of school celebrations because doing so destroys
the significance of both festivals.

Coffin, Tristram P. *The Book of Christmas Folklore*. New
York: Seabury Press, 1973.

Coffin examines the origins of Christmas as a festival
and some of its associated elements. He emphasizes the
survivals theory but makes a few psychologically-oriented
remarks. There are some good comments on Christmas carols
as the author notes the remarkable similarity of narratives
surrounding their composition. Coffin also comments on the
influence of Dickens and the laissez-faire attitude toward
Christmas.

Colditz, S. "Das Weihnachtsfest in Geschichte, Brauchtum
und Sprache." *Müttersprache*, 76 (1966), 353–64.

This is another short essay on Christmas customs and
history.

Cole, Nyla J., et al. "Christmas Reactions." *American Prac-
titioner*, 10 (1959), 2180–84.

The authors describe some mental and emotional reactions
to Christmas, but of greater interest is the section on
"Contemporary Christmas," which outlines general holiday
rituals in the United States: (1) Everyone should celebrate;
(2) Everyone should renew family ties; (3) Everyone should
receive gifts; (4) Everyone should have a Christmas dinner;
(5) Everyone should have a Christmas tree; and (6) Everyone
must be happy. The culture also allows individual or collective deviations. One can be the first, the biggest,
the most spectacular, the loudest, the most different, but
when circumstances block the fulfillment of the basic ritual
components of Christmas, conflict, psychological or social,
is bound to ensue.

Collins, Gary R. "'Tis the Season to Be Jolly'--or Melancholy." *Christianity Today*, 18, no. 5 (7 December 1973),
5–6.

Collins's work is a lay article on depression at Christmas.

Collins, Philip. "*Carol* Philosophy, Cheerful Views." *Etudes Anglaises*, 23 (1970), 158-67.

Dickens contributed a great deal toward the idealization of Christmas, especially with regard to the importance of food. Collins reviews Dickens's Christmas writings; Dickens's concern for Christmas was not a pose--he was home-loving and Christmas was the best time of year for him. He honored the ordinary joys and sorrows of ordinary people. Much of his sense of life accumulates around Christmas. He emphasizes primarily pre-Christian aspects, which provide a splash of color and extravagance in a dreary world.

Colson, Elizabeth. *The Makah Indians*. Manchester, England: Manchester University Press, 1953.

In discussing the natives' adaptations of European customs to suit the whims of the whites, Colson notes that some essential elements are retained. The Christmas tree (pp. 17-18) has been adopted but has acquired some of the characteristics of a potlatch. Goods are hung on it and given away as "presents," but there is competition to see who can give the most and also who can give the biggest Christmas parties.

Commission on Religion in the Public Schools, American Association of School Administrators. *Religion in the Public Schools*. N.p.: American Association of School Administrators, 1964.

Pp. 31-37 cover the role of Christmas in public schools. The holiday should not be ignored, but each school should develop its own approach based on the needs of its students. Explicitly religious manifestations should be handled with great care, if at all.

Conybeare, Fred C. "History of Christmas." *American Journal of Theology*, 3 (1899), 1-21.

Conybeare presents a thorough historical survey of the origins of the ecclesiastical celebration of Christmas, especially as it relates to Epiphany. Emphasis is placed on the diadic relationship between the physical birth of Jesus Christ and his spiritual rebirth (Epiphany).

Count, Earl. *4000 Years of Christmas*. New York: H. Schuman, 1948.

This is a general historical overview of the development of Christmas and its elements. Count discusses Christmas

activities as originally belonging to New Year's. Especially interesting is the description of the Christian adaptation of the Roman Saturnalia. Count also traces the spread
of some of the originally pagan Christmas customs from
Mesopotamia to Christian Europe. One branch was routed
through Greece, but other customs spread via Germanic tribes
in the Danube region before reaching Western Europe.

Cowie, L.W., and John Selwyn Gummer. *The Christian Calendar*.
    London: Weidenfeld and Nicolson, 1974.

Pp. 21-27 investigate the historical development of
Christmas. Particular attention is paid to the history
of Christmas cards and to secular figures such as Santa
Claus.

Cox, Gordon. "The Christmas Carolling Tradition of Green's
    Harbour, Trinity Bay, Newfoundland." *Canadian Folk Music
    Journal*, 3 (1975), 3-10.

In contrast to most Christmas carol studies, which re-
strict themselves to text reporting or minimal description
of the carolling event, Cox presents a brief but impressive
analysis of carolling's various functions. For some people
it is a deeply emotional experience with profound religious
overtones. Food exchange is involved and other social
solidarity and integrative functions are manifested. The
incorporation of new values is apparent along with a staunch
defense of some of the event's traditional elements such
as choice and order of songs, time of performance, and
lack of musical accompaniment.

————. *Folk Music in a Newfoundland Outport*. National
    Museum of Man Mercury series, paper no. 32. Ottawa:
    National Museum of Canada, Canadian Centre for Folk
    Culture Studies, 1980.

Two chapters in Cox's book deal with Christmas carolling
traditions. He reviews the carolling practices of England,
Wales, and Newfoundland, then launches into a discussion
of the adaptations various communities have made in reper-
toire, manner of performance, and composition of carolling
group. An intensive musicological analysis is followed by
some functional remarks involving the use of carolling as
a religious vigil, a social response to the confinement
of the sick and elderly, an attempt to keep the community
in touch with the past, and also a means of strengthening
present community ties. Carolling also serves as an emotional release by reminding people of their childhoods.

Cox stresses that carolling is a "musical occasion," not just a matter of texts and music.

Cox, Harvey. "What Are We Celebrating and Why?" *Redbook*, 126, no. 2 (December, 1965), 40–41, 133–34.

Cox explores the emphasis in Christmas celebrations on either secular/commercial or ecclesiastical observances. He proposes that each observer celebrate in his/her own way, a way that will make Jesus' birth and life personally meaningful. No single definition provides *the* meaning for everyone.

Coyle, F.A., and Russell Eisenman. "Santa Claus Drawings by Negro and White Children." *Journal of Social Psychology*, 80 (1970), 201–5.

White children color pictures of Santa with white or sharp colors while black children use colors more indicative of skin tone: white, black, or brown.

Craddick, R.A. "Size of Santa Claus Drawings as a Function of Time, Before and After Christmas." *Journal of Psychological Studies*, 12 (1961), 121–25.

Craddick tests Salley and Haigh's 1957 study of children's drawings of Santa Claus. The drawings became bigger as Christmas approached but remained large even twelve days after Christmas, indicating some residual Christmas spirit. College freshmen drew larger pictures and saw Santa as a symbol; children saw him as an actual giver.

Crawford, William H. *Holidays in Wales*. New York: Oxford University Press, 1950.

Crawford's book is mainly a description of carol-singing in Wales. He does provide some detail about the practice's historical development, believing it to have developed from the old "Plygain," the singing of three Christmas Masses which evolved into Protestant all-night singing on Christmas Eve.

Crippen, T.G. *Christmas and Christmas Lore*. London: Blackie and Son, 1923; rpt. Detroit: Gale, 1971.

This extensive survey of Christmas folklore is mainly descriptive but includes considerable material on the origins of folk customs.

Crooke, W. "Christmas Candles." *Folk-Lore*, 28 (1917), 106.

This note, one of the few efforts devoted exclusively to Christmas candles, offers few interpretive comments.

Curtis, George William. "Christmas." *Harper's*, 68, no. 403 (December, 1883), 3-16.

Curtis discusses the blending of Christian and non-Christian customs and also the influence of the Puritans, Martin Luther, and Charles Dickens on Christmas celebrations.

Cusack, Frank. *The Australian Christmas*. Melbourne: Heinemann, 1966.

This mainly descriptive volume is the only substantial work available on Christmas in Australia.

Davenport-Adams, W.H. *Scenes of the Olden Time*. London: Nelson and Sons, 1874.

Although mainly descriptive/historical, this work does contain some poetic but not overly sentimental comments on the importance of snow at Christmas. Snow is "the only thing in Nature which gives the idea of uniformity" (p. 139).

Davis, Billie. "A Migrant Child's Christmas: A Chance to Give and Grow." *New Generation*, 56, no. 3 (1974), 1, 3-4.

Migrant farmworkers' children have few sanctioned and structured outlets for expressing joy and appreciation. They should have an opportunity to give in order to quiet guilts and cover inadequacies. Society should make an effort to help the poor celebrate Christmas.

Davis, J. "Gifts and the U.K. Economy." *Man*, 7 (1972), 408-29.

Davis provides a good economic analysis. While not expressly about Christmas, Christmas gift exchanges are used as illustration. Gift production is similar to other forms of business, but suffers from problems related to seasonality. Comparisons are made between the British gift economy and primitives' gift exchange.

Davis, Susan G. "'Making Night Hideous': Christmas Revelry and Public Order in Nineteenth-Century Philadelphia." *American Quarterly*, 34, no. 2 (1982, in press).

This paper examines the development of the nineteenth-century working class's public celebrations of Christmas in Philadelphia. Despite increasing middle-class emphasis on togetherness and cozy family-oriented celebrations, the holiday street scenes provided a "theatre for antagonism" relating to class, racial, and male-female relationships. Change and conflict rather than tradition and good will were the leitmotifs of street displays. Davis considers the impact of demographics, immigration, industrialization, and labor relations. She also focuses on the youth of many of the celebrants and makes extensive use of the local press's comments on the impact of poor, unemployed young men and how Christmas served as a focal point for their year-round problems.

Davison, Stanley R. "Christmas in Montana." *Montana*, 14, no. 1 (1964), 2-9.

Davison explores the use of various Christmas customs to overcome the problems of bleak frontier life.

Dawson, William Francis. *Christmas: Its Origins and Associations*. London: Elliott Stock, 1902; rpt. Detroit: Gale, 1968.

This is one of the classic historical works on Christmas. Dawson discusses pagan origins of Christmas and then examines in detail Christmas celebrations in various eras of British history, with a few comments on non-British Christmas customs. The preface reveals a profound sense of Christmas as part of an ongoing process, intimately connected with what goes on throughout the year. Dawson's approach to a discussion of pagan elements is also quite perceptive; instead of describing them as merely swallowed up or mutilated by Christianity, he stresses their position as links with the past, with older religions, which were necessary for the new Christians to help make the transition from their previous beliefs.

Dearborn, Dorothy. "Christmas Cards through the Years." *Atlantic Advocate*, 66 (December, 1975), 21-23.

This short article on the history of Christmas cards emphasizes the Victorian period, during which they were developed.

Dearmer, Percy; R. Vaughan Williams; and Martin Shaw. *The Oxford Book of Carols*. London: Oxford University Press, 1928.

The preface to this collection discusses the history of Christmas carols.

Deems, Edward. *Holy-Days and Holidays*. New York and London: Funk and Wagnalls, 1902.

Deems's historical study includes comments on Christmas customs around the world, strikingly odd customs, and Christmas literary pieces and sermons.

Dengler, H.W. "Festivals of Flame and Fire." *American Forests*, 77 (December, 1971), 4-5, 47.

This article presents a general survey of the Yule log's various manifestations in Europe and its historical development.

Dirks, Robert. "Slaves' Holiday." *Natural History*, 84, no. 10 (December, 1975), 84-90.

Dirks provides an extensive discussion of colonial slaves' Christmas celebrations in the Caribbean. More than just occasions for role reversal, the celebrations were often times of revolt. Increased rebelliousness may have resulted because of the greater availability of food after a long season of near starvation. This suggests that man as a physical and social being is synchronized to his environment; rapid change triggers hyperactivity and increased aggressive behavior.

Dölger, J. "Natalis Solis Invicti und das Christliche Weihnachtsfest." *Antike und Christentum*, 6 (1940-1950), 23-30.

Dölger investigates the historical and liturgical relationship between the Mithraic festival of the birth of the sun and the Christian observances of Christmas.

Dorson, Richard. "Yuletide Gift-Givers." *What's New*, no. 215 (1959), 29-33.

In this obscure journal distributed by a pharmaceutical company, Dorson discusses Santa Claus's differences from European Christmas gift-bringing figures. Santa Claus is described as a caricature of Uncle Sam, who embodies the American love of well being, dreams of abundance, and democracy as he visits *every* home and *always* leaves good things. Dorson also mentions European figures and classifies them according to their lightness-white qualities or as creatures of darkness. He then gives general historical information on St. Nicholas (Low Countries, parts of Germany, Austria, Switzerland), St. Martin of Tours (Belgium), the Christchild or *Christkind* (Germany, Austria), the Magi (Spain), the elfin *nisse* (Norway), Befana (Italy), Knecht Rupert (Germany), and Father Christmas (England).

Douglas, George W. *American Book of Days*. New York: H.W. Wilson Co., 1937.

Although mainly descriptive, this book (and its several subsequent editions by different compilers) contain some historical material on Christmas.

Drotman, Gilda. "Take the Crises Out of Christmas." *Learning*, 2, no. 3 (November, 1973), 62-63.

This article questions the legal, moral, and educational propriety of Christmas festivities in public schools. Personal and constitutional rights are being sacrificed to the demands of tradition.

du Tilliot, J.B.L. *Mémoires pour servir à l'histoire de la Fête des Foux*. Geneva: Lausannet, 1751.

This book is an historical survey of the Feast of Fools, often celebrated around Christmastime. It includes songs, poems, theatrical dialogues, and many illustrations.

Duchesne, Louis. *Origines du culte Chrétien*. Paris: E. de Boccard, [1902]. English translation, *Christian Worship*. London: Society for Promising Christian Knowledge, 1903; New York: E. and J.B. Young and Co., 1903.

The book mentions Nativity scenes and Christmas Masses but it is mainly concerned (in the section on Christmas) with the history of fixing the date of Christ's birth.

Duncan, F. "Trees of Christmas-tide in Folk-lore." *Critic*, 47 (1905), 506-9.

Duncan discusses the origins of Christmas greenery in Greek and Druid times.

Duncan, Hugh Salzil. *Symbols in Society*. New York: Oxford University Press, 1968.

Duncan comments on Christmas as a means of breaking down rigid social and economic class barriers and also notes the effects of commercialization.

Dundes, Alan. "Christmas as a Reflection of American Cul-
    ture." *California Monthly*, 78, no. 3 (1967), 9-15.

    This is an excellent, very informative article. Dundes
stresses that the way Americans celebrate Christmas reveals
American values and worldview. Various aspects of Santa
Claus are explored: belief in him as a result of parental
pressure, his overshadowing of Jesus, Santa as a masculine
figure. Also, Santa Claus is always good to children because American parents dislike administering punishment.
Dundes mentions the uniting of religious and secular concepts through Christmas and that it is also a ritual occasion for uniting families. He gives an interesting analysis
(derived from Barnett) of Rudolph the Red-Nosed Reindeer
as an American child's "success dream come true." Dundes's
discussion includes comments on the commercialization of
Christmas; he feels that such an important festival naturally
should reflect capitalist motives.

Dunphy, Hubert M. *Christmas Every Christmas*. Milwaukee:
    Bruce, 1960.

    Although oriented heavily to theology, Dunphy's analysis
is sometimes more broadly applicable. He compares the
Catholic Church's concept of Christmas to its meaning among
the laity. He also suggests ways to improve modern Christmas celebrations by reviving old customs.

Ebon, Martin. *Saint Nicholas: Life and Legend*. New York:
    Harper, 1975.

    This is an excellent historical work on St. Nicholas's
life, death, cult, and development into Christmas gift-
givers such as Santa Claus. Special note is made of the
influence of artist Thomas Nast and the "Yes, Virginia"
editorial on American conceptions of Santa Claus.

Edie, Priscilla D. "Christmas in the Library." *Horn Book*,
    21, no. 6 (November, 1945), 434-48.

    This article discusses books and activities children
find appealing at Christmastime and how they relate to the
overall spirit of Christmas.

Edwards, V.L. "Story of Christmas." *Americas*, 21 (1969),
    18-27.

    Edwards provides a general history with an emphasis on
Latin American Christmas celebrations, Nativity scenes,
and Santa Claus-type figures. He makes an interesting

observation regarding Spain's early conversion to Christianity and its lack of pagan-derived Christmas customs,
in contrast to Scandinavia, which converted far later and
still has a large number of originally pagan customs.

Ehrensvärd, Ulla. *Den Svenska Tomten.* Stockholm: Kungl.
Bibliotekets, 1979.

Tomten is the Swedish counterpart of Santa Claus. This
book discusses its history and forerunners in Swedish
legend.

Eisenbud, Jule. "Negative Reactions to Christmas." *Psychoanalytic Quarterly,* 10 (1941), 639-45.

Eisenbud believes that Christmas is a time when people
are inclined to pursue individual gratification, which is
normally held in check. Both Christmas and New Year's
permit forms of entertainment not usually allowed and
produce a relaxing of the superego. Eisenbud's main discussion involves Santa Claus, who always brings what is
wanted. This is related to clinical examples of penis
envy.

Ellekilde, Hans. *Vor danske Jul gennem Tiderne.* Copenhagen:
G.E.C. Gad, 1943.

Ellekilde's book is one of the major Scandinavian works
on the history of the Northern European Christmas festival.
It begins as an outline of ancient pagan mid-winter customs
and Roman New Year's observances, then covers in detail
Christmas in Denmark in the early and late medieval period,
the impact of Lutheranism, the bourgeois Christmases of
the eighteenth and nineteenth centuries, and, finally,
Christmas in the twentieth century. The middle sections
have a heavy ecclesiastical emphasis, but the others combine
folk and elite, religious and secular songs, customs, etc.

————. "Af julenissens histoire." *Slaegtsgaarden,* n.v.
(1955), 8-13.

This article presents a short history of the Scandinavian
elves/spirits that appear around Christmastime.

Emurian, Ernest K. *Stories of Christmas Carols.* Boston:
W.A. Wilde Co., 1958.

Emurian provides detailed histories of eleven Christmas
carols and thereby presents valuable information on the
history of various aspects of Christmas. For example, his

discussion of "We Three Kings of Orient Are" suggests possible identities for the Magi and offers a consideration of
their role in Christmas narratives and observances. The
carols studied include very popular ones, such as "Silent
Night" and "Joy to the World," as well as some more obscure
ones, such as "As with Gladness Men of Old."

Eskeröd, Albert. *Årets Äring, Etnologiska Studier I Skördena
    och Julens Tro och Sed*. Nordiska Museets Handlingar,
    no. 26. Stockholm: Nordiska Museets, 1947.

Eskeröd's book is mainly concerned with harvest customs,
especially those surrounding the last sheaf, but includes
some information on Christmas traditions that are assumed
to be connected with harvest customs. Eskeröd believes
that most Christmas beliefs and practices deal with "psycho-
biological primary motives--the instinct of self-preservation
and the wish for happiness, the permanently dominating interests at the turn of the year" (p. 366). He stresses
that beliefs and customs "have grown up from the basis of
contemporary techniques of work, the social environment,
and the psychological reactions of the groups concerned"
(p. 368). The volume includes an English summary.

————. "Julhalmen och fruktbarhetsteorierna." *Rig*, 30
    (1947), 16-41.

In this essay, Eskeröd presents a scathing criticism of
early interpretations of Christmas customs involving straw
as a fertility symbol. Unfortunately, his own analysis is
not adequately conveyed, at least not in the English summary. He explains the straw as the "result of dominant
human interests, filling the mind of the farmer especially
at Christmas." What these interests are is not explained,
but they apparently have something to do with the turn of
the year and the supernatural powers of the straw.

Ettlinger, L.D., and R.G. Holloway. *Compliments of the
    Season*. London: Penguin, 1947.

The authors' obscure and short but very perceptive historical and sociological analysis of Christmas cards includes a discussion of origins and the influence of continental New Year's cards, calling cards, and valentines.
The effect of industrialization and machinery on the cards'
production is also covered, as is the relationship between
cards, art, and popular taste, and the improvements of the
postal system as they relate to the sending of Christmas
cards. A brief discussion of the reasons for sending cards
is provided.

Etzioni, Amitai. "Christmas Blues." *Psychology Today*, 10,
   no. 7 (December, 1976), 231.

   Holiday stress is stimulated by expectations involving
   exchange of gifts and love-hate relationships with relatives.
   Strife-ridden Christmases are reminders of deviance from
   the American ideal. Most people suffer from some degree
   of Christmas blues.

Evans, George Ewart. "Christmas Light and Dark." *New
   Society*, 8 (1966), 950.

   Christmas is a contest between good and bad, light and
   dark. This is often seen in the symbols associated with
   Christmas: the Yule log is an assist to the sun; the hunting
   of the wren is a fertility symbol, as is the Mari Lwyd
   observance in Wales. Mari Lwyd involves a person dressed
   as a horse who visits houses and is not allowed to enter
   because he represents Death, but is not turned away because
   that would anger Death. Ewart also discusses the effect of
   economics. In the nineteenth century, Christmas was viewed
   with little more respect than a Sunday because it fell
   during a bad time of year for farmers. This contradicts
   the opinion of other writers that Christmas is held at an
   excellent time of year because it falls after harvest-time,
   when there are few demands on agricultural workers in terms
   of outside chores.

Ewert, Cagnar, ed. *Swedish Christmas*. Gothenberg: Tre
   Tryckare, 1955.

   This is a catch-all book including a survey of the origin
   and development of Christmas customs, with some mystical
   explanations, a personal psychological analysis of Christmas
   candles, and a discussion of Lapp Christmas customs.

Faye, P.L. "Christmas Festivals of the Cupeno." *American
   Anthropologist*, 30 (1928), 651-58.

   Faye's article is mainly descriptive but concludes that
   Cupeno life is similar to that in villages in southern
   Europe where the village fiesta is replacing old types of
   exchanges of courtesies between clans. Spanish and Catholic
   acculturative factors are at work among Indians in the
   American Southwest.

Fehr, Laurence. "J. Piaget and S. Claus: Psychology Makes
   Strange Bedfellows." *Psychological Reports*, 39 (1976),
   740-42.

Fehr discusses the cessation of belief in Santa Claus as the result of the development of logical thinking, the reaching of the concrete operational stage of development.

Fehrle, Eugen. *Deutsche Feste und Volksbrauche*. Leipzig and Berlin: B.G. Leubner, 1916.

Section 10 deals with Christmas, in a descriptive fashion but with some historical material on origins of customs and the Christmas festival.

Feilburg, H.F. *Jul, Allsjaelstiden Hedensk, Kristen Julefest*. 2 vols. Copenhagen: Rosenkilde og Bagger, 1962.

Volume 1 deals with Christian and non-Christian obser-vances of All Souls Day and their connections with pagan Nordic mid-winter celebrations. Danish, Norwegian, and Swedish customs are reviewed. Then the analysis shifts to the general development of Christmas and its legends (Magi, adoration of the animals), followed by a description of Christmas in various parts of the world: the United States, Korea, Constantinople, China, on a warship, in jail, among the lonely. Volume 2 discusses the "dark" side of Christ-mas, that is, concepts of the spirits of the dead and the dangers of the night. Beliefs, omens, the tree, and pro-cessions receive special attention.

Feist, Sigmund. "Die Etymologie des Festnamens Jul." *Zeit-schrift für vergleichenden Sprachforschung*, 51 (1923), 143–44.

This is a linguistically-oriented historical analysis of the words "Jul" and "Weihnacht," the Scandinavian and German words for Christmas.

Fiedler, Fritz. "Das Weihnachtsfest in England vor und bei Dickens." *Archiv für das Studium der neueren Sprachens*, 141 (1921), 59–78.

Fiedler presents abundant material on the development and kinds of songs sung at Christmas (carols, hymns, wassail) but also explores the effects of Puritan repression of Christmas and the holiday's resurgent popularity in the nineteenth century due to increasing interest in antiquities and the effects of the writing of Dickens, Scott, Irving, and many articles in the popular press.

Finckh, Alice H. "In the Candle's Glow." *American-German Review*, 14, no. 2 (December, 1947), 4–6.

Finckh provides a history of the Christmas tree in the
United States, including its ornaments, such as candles.

Fink, Hans. "Der Adventkranz zu seiner Herkunft und Ver-
breitung." *Der Schlern*, 45 (1971), 23-33.

Fink discusses the origin and dissemination of the
Advent wreath.

Firestone, Bea. "Christmas and Hanukkah in the Public
Schools--One Community's Dilemma." *Jewish Education*,
37 (1967), 180-87.

Firestone surveys the reactions of Jewish and gentile
educators and PTA parents to the celebration of Christmas
in a Kansas public school system. Hanukkah celebrations
are used to balance the Christmas observances, but many
Jews feel this overemphasizes a relatively minor Jewish
celebration. Although no direct comments from Jewish
students are provided, the article concludes that Jewish
children will be hurt by Christian celebrations even if
they emphasize cultural rather than religious themes.

Firestone, Melvin. "Christmas Mumming and Symbolic Interaction." *Ethos*, 6 (1978), 92-113.

Following a survey of previous anthropological and
sociological studies of mumming, Firestone gives his own
symbolically-oriented assessment. The analysis focuses
on mumming in and of itself rather than as a custom
specific to Christmas.

Flusser, Walter. "Provenzalische Weihnachten, eine volks-
kundliche-literar-historische Untersuchung." *Zeitschrift
für Romanische Philologie*, 51 (1931), 1-58, 129-93.

Flusser presents a collection, description, and history
of many German folk customs of Christmas, including Advent
practices, Nativity scenes, songs, Epiphany spirits, and
so forth.

Fogel, Edwin Miller. *Twelvetide*. Pennsylvania-German Folklore Society Publication, vol. 6. Allentown, Pa.:
Pennsylvania-German Folklore Society, 1941.

This brief look at the winter holiday season, its customs,
and their history emphasizes Pennsylvania-German examples.

Foley, Daniel J. *The Christmas Tree*. Philadelphia: Chilton,
1960.

Foley's book is mainly an historical and descriptive study of the Christmas tree with additional material on the general history of Christmas. His research is thorough, and is supplemented with illustrations and photographs. He includes discussions of the Paradise tree, the Christmas tree in Germany, England, and America, the Christmas tree as a business venture, decorations and tinsel, and narratives.

Fortún, Julia Elena. "La Navidad en al ámbito chuquisaqueño." *Cuaderno de la Sociedad folklórica de Bolivia*, no. 1 (1952), 13-23.

Frazer, Sir James George. *The Golden Bough: A Study in Myth and Religion*, 13 vols. London: Macmillan, 1890. (Several subsequent editions, some abridged.)

References to Christmas and Christmas customs are scattered throughout this work. Among Frazer's comments are a discussion of the influence of Mithraism, pagan origins of various beliefs and practices (e.g., the Yule log), and the early Catholic Church's reasons for moving the observance of Christ's birth from January 6 to December 25.

Freemantle, Anne. "Christmas in Literature." *Commonweal*, 43 (1945), 185-88.

Freemantle briefly surveys authors who have utilized Christmas themes in their works, including Shakespeare, Milton, Hardy, Browning, Alcott, and Tolstoy.

Fri, James L. "This Business of Christmas: Toys." *Current History*, 47 (1937), 53-56.

Fri looks at economic trends that influence the availability and assortment of toys at Christmas. He also explores manufacturers' trends and the transformation from giving novelty presents to educational toys.

Fritzssch, Karl Ewald. "Zur Geschichte der erzgebirgischen Weihnachtspyramide." *Sächsische Heimatblätter*, 12 (1966), 474-99.

The author presents a history of Christmas pyramids, triangular cupboard-like items with shelves for figures, fruits, nuts, and gifts.

Gailey, Alan. *Irish Folk Drama*. Cork: Mercier Press, 1969.

Gailey evaluates Christmas mumming practices in terms of their relationship to other life-cycle dramas such as those

associated with the year's quarter-days, weddings, and
wakes. Christmas/mid-winter is a point of seasonal crises.
The plays depict the idea of death and rebirth, miming the
human life cycle and assisting nature in the unfolding of
the seasons.

Gaillard, J. "Noël: Memoria ou mystère." *Maison-Dieu*, 59
    (1959), 37-59.

The author examines two viewpoints on Christmas, as a
memoria, or commemoration of an historical event, and as
a liturgical celebration of the mystery of the Incarnation
of Christ.

Galanti, A. "Christmas for First Generation Americans."
    American Home, 23, no. 1 (December, 1939), 49-50, 64.

Galanti discusses the experience of one immigrant family
in adopting American and English "Christmasisms," then
realizing that they want to retain some old-country customs
as well. The article provides no in-depth sociological
analysis of their situation or any indication of how wide-
spread it is.

Galdston, Richard. "Coping with Behavior Problems; Why
    Holiday Traditions Play a Vital Role in the Lives of
    Children." *Parents Magazine*, 51, no. 12 (December,
    1976), 24.

The holiday season helps children gain a sense of continuity and community which is essential to emotional
development. Customary practices help counter mood swings
caused by mingled feelings of expectation and anxiety.
"It is a time of year when we honor the value of our relationships to one another, to our shared past and our
future."

Gastoué, Amedée. *Noël*. Paris: Librairie Bloud, 1907. 2nd
    edition (1908) is entitled *Noël. Origines et Développe-
    ments de la fête*.

Gastoué emphasizes the questions surrounding the establishment of the date of Christmas, the development of
liturgy, Nativity plays, and folk Christmas celebrations,
particularly Christmas carols.

Geiger, Paul. "Weihnachtsfest und Weihnachtsbaum." *Schweizer-
    isches Archiv für Volkskunde*, 27 (1939/40), 229-54.

Geiger's well-written article explores the various combinations of Christian, Roman, and pagan European elements

of Christmas. Of particular importance are customs associated with death and the return of the dead and with prosperity and fertility, not to mention light cults. The Christmas tree custom is used to illustrate the various aspects.

Gennep, Arnold van. *Le Cycle des douze jours.* Vol. VII of his *Manuel de folklore français contemporain.* Paris: Picard, 1958.

This two-part work contains descriptions of various Christmastime customs throughout France, with special emphasis on activities involving fire and light. The brief introduction stresses the importance of the family on this occasion and the major role Christmas plays in the French celebratory tradition. Christmas Eve and Day are just the culmination, however, of the winter cycle of festivities. The *Cycle des douze jours* covers roughly the period from Christmas Eve to Epiphany but can start much earlier with a preparation period encompassing most of late autumn. Van Gennep provides historical information on the different dates assigned to Christmas and New Year's as well as data on the various names given to Christmas. He also emphasizes the importance of the days before important events (e.g., Christmas Eve) as a time of preparation before encountering the sacred or divine.

Ghéon, Henri. *Noël! Noël!* Paris: Ernest Flammarian, 1935.

Directed to a popular audience, this book includes many photographs and illustrations along with commentary on the origins, history, and liturgy of Christmas, as well as art, legends, songs, nativity scenes, foods, and customs.

Gilst, A.P. van. *Sinterklaus en het Sinterklaasfest, Geschiedenis en Folklore.* Veenendaal: Uitgeverij Midgaard, 1961.

This work is a descriptive/historical study of St. Nicholas and Santa Claus. It examines their pagan precursors, Christian saints, and folk legends and customs surrounding the character and his feast day.

Ginalska, Maria Polskie. *Bože Narodzenie.* London: B. Świderski, 1961.

This is an extensive examination of Christmas in Poland: its history, decorations, poetry, Nativity scenes, and mumming practices.

Glassie, Henry. *All Silver and No Brass: An Irish Christmas Mumming.* Bloomington: Indiana University Press, 1975.

To sum up Glassie's sensitive work in just a few lines is almost impossible. He reports four conversations with residents of Ballymenone, a community in Northern Ireland, on the topic of Christmas mumming. Although mumming no longer occurs, Glassie stresses the effects past mumming practices have on the people's behavioral reality. He reinterprets the survivalistic aspects of mumming, for although it is a fragment of the past, it remains part of behavior in Ballymenone, which Glassie wants to investigate. He provides fine functional and performance-oriented assessments, but most important, he relates mumming to its place within the cycle of the year and as a part of the Christmas season, its (former) highpoint. There is still room for further study, but Glassie accomplishes more than many of the other mumming researchers.

Goepfert, Günter, ed. *Alpenländische Weihnacht.* Munich: Süddeutscher Verlag, 1970.

This is mainly a collection of poetry, song lyrics, and short prose pieces on Christmas. It includes beautiful photographs of Nativity scenes and individual figures.

Goldin, Grace. "Christmas-Chanukah—December Is the Cruelest Month." *Commentary,* 10 (1950), 416-25.

This is a fairly good article that centers on one family's problems at Christmastime with being Jewish in a predominantly Christian community. Goldin stresses how Jewish parents are tempted to overdo Hanukkah to compensate for the lack of a Christmas for their children. She provides interesting information on children's reactions to the situation.

Goodbar, Octavia. "This Business of Christmas: Cards." *Current History,* 47 (1937), 56-58.

Goodbar reviews the history of Christmas as a legal American holiday, then discusses the development of the American greeting-card industry. She sees the Christmas card as a discharge of social obligations that formerly were filled by writing long letters.

Grigson, Geoffrey. "Ox and Ass in the Christmas Story." *Country Life,* 134 (1963), 1454-56.

Grigson looks at the history of the ox and ass in the Christmas story and their portrayal in paintings of the Nativity.

Grolman, H.O.A. *Les Traditions magico-religieuses des fêtes calendaires.* Proceedings of the Third Session of the Institut International d'Anthropologie, Amsterdam, 1927. Paris: Actes du Congrès International d'Anthropologie, 1928, pp. 525-30.

This article covers the pagan origins of certain festivals, including winter solstice/Christmas observances. Grolman emphasizes the sun as an important factor in the celebrations and in determining their dates.

Groöt, Adriaan D. de. "Sint Nicholaas." *Nederlandes Tijdschrift voor de Psychologie en haar Grendsgebieden*, 2 (1947), 520-35.

This article is the forerunner of de Groöt's book (see below). His thesis is that St. Nicholas should be viewed as the patron saint not only of children but also of *kinderzegen*, which includes maidens, lovers, marriage, conception, unborn children, and birth, that is, everything connected with children in the biological cycle.

————. *St. Nicholas: A Psychoanalytic Study of His History and Myth.* The Hague and Paris: Mouton, 1965.

De Groöt's excellent work concentrates on the European gift-bringer, but he says the American Santa Claus has features similar to St. Nicholas's. De Groöt believes that through the specialization and Christianization of general pagan fertility cults, St. Nicholas became the unofficial patron saint of *kinderzegen* (see the preceding citation). He reviews the mythical elements surrounding the saint, the history of his Christian cult, and the pagan contributions to it. The latter part of the work is extremely psychoanalytic. There are discussions of Freud's and Jung's theories, which are then applied to St. Nicholas. There is a good discussion of why St. Nicholas is the patron saint of sailors, stressing the sexual implications of a ship in port. The book concludes with a summary of a paper by Fritz Redl entitled "Free—and Not So Free—Associations after Reading de Groöt's *Sinterklaas*." Redl provides a sociological interpretation of St. Nicholas with comments on his manifestation of the social reality of justice, bureaucracy, authority, and truth. He criticizes de Groöt for not touching on how St. Nicholas affects our time in terms of human behavior and development, aggression, fear of retaliation, sin, and forgiveness. Redl also believes that St. Nicholas is highly desexualized and that he represents a cluster of drives.

Gross, J. "The Season's Greetings." *New Statesman*, 64, no.
    1659 (28 December 1962), 935.

    Gross presents a brief sociological study of Christmas
    cards. They originated in the Victorian period, when people
    had to bear the brunt of harsh and rapid social change.
    Life was colorless and uncertain, so fantasies had to be
    bright and secure. The more competitive the society, the
    more need there was for festivals giving the illusion of
    good will. Sending cards was a way of playing "happy
    family" by remote control. It was also a means of keeping
    in touch with immigrants. Gross points out how the one-
    time popularity of Dickens scenes on cards parallels the
    use of Disney motifs today.

Gross, Leonard. "Jews and Christmas: To Observe or Not?
    From a New Generation, a New Answer." *Look*, 29, no. 26
    (28 December 1965), 22-24.

    American Jews of the 1960s rejected the assimilationist
    ways of their parents. The Jew is psychologically free to
    celebrate Christmas or not, but may embellish Hanukkah.
    (Ed. note: This embellishment may signal that they are not
    psychologically free at all.) The Jew is rediscovering
    what he has tried to forget. See Witt's article below for
    a 1939 discussion of the same problem.

Gwynne, Walker. *The Christian Year.* New York: Longmans,
    Green & Co., 1915; rpt. Detroit: Gale, 1971.

    The development of the Christian year, including Christ-
    mas, is traced from its beginnings in older rituals and
    festivals.

Hadfield, Miles, and John Hadfield. *The Twelve Days of
    Christmas.* Boston: Little, Brown and Co., 1961.

    The book concentrates on the origins and symbolism of
    the Christmas festival and its customs (e.g., greenery,
    gifts, cards). Associated events such as Boxing Day,
    St. John's Day (December 27), Childermas (December 28),
    Epiphany, and the medieval celebration of the Feast of
    Fools are also covered. There is an interesting discussion
    of the identities of the Magi. No bibliography, and few
    references, are provided.

Hagstrom, Warren O. "What Is the Meaning of Santa Claus?"
    American Sociologist, 2 (1966), 248-52.

    Hagstrom presents various approaches to the analysis of
    belief in Santa Claus, including animism, solar mythology,

and the search for historical origins. He believes that Santa Claus is a father figure who is at ease in giving affection, but Hagstrom also explores the Marxist interpretations of Santa as an expression of distress and an opiate of childhood. In addition, the Durkheimian view is presented; Santa is a sacred figure whose belief is related to a set of rites. As other Western societies and their family systems become more like the United States, Santa and other gift-giving figures will change accordingly. Hagstrom maintains that "Santa Claus is simultaneously a father figure, a child control technique and a symbolic representation of affect in small family groups."

Halpert, Herbert, and G.M. Story, eds. *Christmas Mumming in Newfoundland*. Toronto: University of Toronto Press, 1969.

This anthology is a good example of the analytical treatment of mumming. Most analyses of mumming, including those in Halpert and Story's book, do not relate the performances to the season in which they occur. Instead, comments are directed toward texts, history, description, structure, or relation to general social structures.

Hare, Kenneth. "Christmas Folklore." *Quarterly Review*, 264-65, no. 523 (December, 1935), 31-46.

Although this is basically an origins-oriented article, Hare does present some good background data on winter festivals in pre-Christian England, the significance of the boar's head as traditional English Christmas food, and the cult of the Yule log. Lights, superstitions, mumming, and greenery are also examined, and there is some discussion of the Puritan repression of Christmas.

Harris, Monford. "Christmas and Hanukkah: Two Structurings of the World." *Jewish Frontier*, 43 (December, 1976), 19-21.

Christmas is a major "Christian" feast; Hanukkah is not a major Jewish feast. The celebrations are radically different and mutually exclusive structurings of the world, for Christmas involves enchantment and timelessness while Hanukkah is concerned with history (specifically, a battle), the purity of the Jews, and the rejection of an enchanted world.

Harrison, Michael. *The Story of Christmas, Its Growth and Development from the Earliest Times*. London: Odhams Press, 1951.

Harrison's initial emphasis is on pagan origins (European, Jewish, Roman), Christianity's influence on British
winter observances, and the subsequent development of
Christmas against the backdrop of general historical eras.
Specific customs such as the Christmas card, Father Christmas, and Nativity scenes are then discussed, followed by a
section describing Christmas celebrations in Australia,
Austria, Germany, Scandinavia, France, Italy, and Spain.

Hartke, Wilhelm. *Über Jahrespunkt und Feste, Insbesondere
das Weihnachtsfest*. Berlin: Akademie, 1956.

There is a heavy emphasis on ecclesiastical documents and
dogma in Hartke's book. He explores the early history of
Christmas, New, Year's, and Epiphany, contributing some
interesting data on possible Egyptian origins. He then
covers the significance of Epiphany and the process of
establishing December 25 as the date of Christ's birth.

Hayakawa, S.I. "Response to Shlien's 'Santa Claus: The
Myth in America.'" *Etc., A Review of General Semantics*,
16 (1950), 399.

Hayakawa is strongly opposed to the fostering of belief
in Santa Claus. He feels that there might be better ways
of "utilizing the sacredness of the child in our culture
than the present 'hocus-pocus.'"

Hayden, A. Eustace. "Christmas: A Symbol." *Religious
Humanism*, 11 (1977), 230-36.

Hayden reviews the development of Christmas and its
symbols, providing some new data and putting forth some
rather obvious misconceptions about previous research.
The emphasis is on the Christianization of pagan customs.
He sees Christmas as a celebration of a new year, which
means new life, hope, and life after death. Hayden also
advocates a reorientation of Christmas symbolism to emphasize joy, personal development, comradeship, and creative
work.

Heindel, Max. *The Mystical Interpretation of Christmas*.
Oceanside, Ca.: Rosicrucian Fellowship, 1925.

This pamphlet is mainly a theological/inspirational work
with heavy emphasis on equivalencies between Christ's birth
and the return of the sun. Christmas is viewed as a time
of influx for spiritual life.

Hervey, Thomas Kibble. *The Book of Christmas; Descriptive of the Customs, Ceremonies, Traditions, Superstitions, Fun, Feeling, and Festivities of the Christmas Season.* London: W. Spooner, 1836.

Hervey's book is mainly descriptive but covers many customs and days of the Christmas season. He offers a review of the history of the holiday and some perceptive comments on the feeling of Christmas and the reasons for its popularity, at least in the mid-nineteenth century.

Hill, C.R. "Christmas Card Selection as Unobtrusive Measures." *Journalism Quarterly*, 46 (1969), 511-14.

Christmas cards offer the opportunity to measure attitudes about Christmas. In a sample of cards from 1967 to 1968, 24 percent had religious themes (especially of the Madonna and Child), and 76 percent were non-religious, suggesting that Christmas has lost its religious vigor.

Hirsch, Emil G. "How the Jew Regards Christmas." *Ladies Home Journal*, 24, no. 1 (December, 1906), 10.

In this brief editorial Hirsch emphasizes commonalities between Hanukkah and Christmas (e.g., the importance of lights and children), but he does not want Hanukkah to become Christmas. Jews should be happy for Christians on their day but not try to copy them.

Höfler, Max. *Weihnachtsgebäcke.* Vienna: Verlag des Vereines für österreichische Volkskunde, 1905.

This is an historical and comparative study of Christmas cookies and breads in Germanic countries. Höfler discusses the relationship of the foods to All Saints/Souls Day and death/life cults. He includes many photographs and illustrations of molds, cookie stamps, and the finished products.

Holder, Judith, and Alison Harding. *Christmas Fare.* Secaucus, N.J.: Chartwell, 1976.

Intended for a popular audience, this book provides interesting comments on the history and use of English Christmas foods, including mincemeat, roast goose, candies, gingerbread, plum pudding, wassail, and twelfth cake.

Holderness, Graham. "Image in *A Christmas Carol*." *Etudes Anglaises*, 32 (1979), 28-45.

Holderness asserts that Dickens's story succeeds because of its use of imagination. He reviews other criticism and

summarizes some of the comments made about Christmas and
Dickens.

Hole, Christina. *British Folk Customs*. London: Hutchinson,
    1976.

    Hole provides a general description and history of Christ-
mas cards, Nativity scenes, gifts, and greenery.

————. *Christmas and Its Customs: A Brief Study*. London:
    Bell, 1957.

    Hole's historical work is oriented toward children, but
it does give a good overview of Christmas celebrations.

Hommel, Rudolf. "On the Trail of the First Christmas Tree."
    Pennsylvania Dutchman, 1, no. 21 (December, 1949), 1.

    This article offers a brief summary of the history of
the Christmas tree with an emphasis on its use in the United
States, especially in Philadelphia.

Hoover, Earl R. "Benjamin Hanbly's Famous Christmas Song 'Up
    on the Housetop.'" *Musician, Journal of Musical History*,
    3, no. 3 (1965), 48-51.

    Hoover discusses how Hanbly's song drifted into oral
circulation and underwent change.

Howell, Elmo. "William Faulkner's 'Christmas Gift.'" *Ken-
    tucky Folklore Record*, 13 (1967), 37-40.

    Howell discusses the origins of the traditional greeting
"Christmas gift," which Faulkner adapted for use in *The
Sound and the Fury*. Howell believes it reflects the relaxation of decorum between master and servant that occurs
during the holiday season.

Huck, Gabe. "Keeping Christmas: Family Ritual for Celebrating."
    New Catholic World, 218 (1975), 268-73.

    Christmas is a festival, a work of art in time. It is
a crucial moment in the rhythm of life as it catches
drooping, even despairing spirits. The holiday was created
out of need and imagination. Christmas rituals should
stress a sense of security, identity, belonging, and give
symbolic expression to our feelings and convictions.

Hudon, J. "Christmas, Its Legends and Lore." *Westminster
    Review*, 16 (1905), 676-85.

Hudon makes some interesting if not very academic comments on the purpose of Christmas.

Huekin, Gordon. "Christmas in the City." *Guildhall Studies in London History*, 3 (1978), 164-74.

Huekin discusses late medieval Christmas customs and notes changes during the Reformation and later revivals of seasonal activities. He includes a discussion of early street decorations.

Hyams, E. "Countryside--Evergreens Associated with Christmas." *New Statesman*, 66 (1963), 923.

Hyams's essay is an average article on the origins of Christmas greenery.

Ingersoll, Ernest. "Under the Mistletoe: The Legends and Significance of Christmas Greens." *Chautauquan*, 12 (1890), 335-39.

Using data from comparative religion and mythology, the author surveys the history of Christmas greenery, particularly holly and mistletoe.

Isambert, François André. "La Fête et les fêtes." *Sociologica Religiosa*, 11 (1968), 41-58.

Isambert discusses medieval religious festivals. They were communal experiences, often representing chaos and creation. Christmas is used as an illustration for his comments.

————. *La Fin de l'année. Etude sur les fêtes de Noël et de Nouvel An à Paris*. Paris: Société des Amis du Centre d'Etudes Sociologiques, 1976.

According to Isambert, Christmas began as a religious occasion but is now primarily an occasion to honor childhood, one's family, and the feeling of hope. This is a thorough study of Christmas as a social phenomenon, including an inventory of elements composing the festival, their functions and significance, and the intersection of festivity, religion, and popular culture. Isambert also comments on the general theory of festivity, observing that the debate on the subject has been too restricted to sacred festivals and that profane ones should be duly considered.

Jaakola, Kaisu. *Muuttuva Joulu: Kansatieteelinen Tutkimus (The Changing Christmas: An Ethnological Study)*. Helsinki:

Suomen Muinaisamuistoyhdistys, 1977.

Jaakola's study was conducted in a Swedish-speaking area
of Finland. She wanted to determine which customs associated
with Christmas were language-specific and determine quanti-
tatively what is and is not common to Finnish Christmas
customs. She also wanted to look at innovations in observances
and see how they spread. Some interesting comments are made
on the influence of the press and on attitudes toward church
bazaars. She concludes with a discussion of the values she
finds encoded in Christmas symbols, which are: hedonic
(good tastes, smells), vitalic (mental health, removal of
stress), aesthetic, religious, patriotic, and social (preser-
vation of hierarchy creating and sustaining identity). She
concludes that "Society changes Christmas, although very
slowly. Christmas does not attempt to change society. It
attempts to retain what has already been achieved" (p. 357).
It is an escape ritual. One day a year is dedicated to
religion (in part) to alleviate the stress that accumulates
from not believing in religion the rest of the year, although
society would like to believe that it does.

Jack, Bertha Francis. "The Rise and Development of Christmas
     Customs and Festivals." M.A. Thesis, George Peabody
     College for Teachers, 1931.

Jack traces pagan and Christian customs, then provides a
brief outline of how the customs can be used for school
pageants. Such use, she hopes, will reduce commercialization.

James, E.O. *Seasonal Feasts and Festivals*. New York: Barnes
     and Noble, 1961.

Comments on Christmas scattered throughout the book are
confined to the usual origins material. There are some
good observations about mummers plays and the Feast of
Fools. While not directly related to Christmas, the early
part of the book presents a theory of the emergence of
seasonal rituals based on the need for food.

Janvier, T.A. *Christmas Kalends of Provence*. New York and
     London: Harper, 1902.

This is a purely descriptive but beautifully written
work.

Jekels, Ludwig. "The Psychology of the Festival of Christmas."
     International Journal of Psychoanalysis, 17 (1936), 57-72.

This excellent article begins with an analysis of why December 25 was chosen as Christmas Day. Since Christ's date of birth could not be arrived at through historical logic, the choice was influenced by religious emotion and conformed to modes of mythological thinking. As Christ conquered the old order of belief, so his day must represent this ousting. Christmas represents father-son rivalry, as there is love and respect for Christ and God but fear as well. Christ was a man, so the Nativity was an assertion of his democracy. It brought the Church closer to the people, a response to the popular demand that people's experiences be translated into terms of the super-personal. This is a difficult article to read, but it gives considerable attention to the psychological writing on Christmas. Many of Jekels's ideas are obscured by his theological arguments, and he gives no citations for his quotations.

Jelinkova, Miriam. "Christmas in Bohemia--Traditional and Present Day." *Lore and Language*, 2 (1970), 9-10.

The author provides a brief assessment of changes in Christmas in Czechoslovakia since the Communist takeover. Many customs remain unchanged, and Christmas appears to be the only major traditional festival to have survived the social and economic upheavals.

Johnson, Leslie Dent. "Classical Origins of Christmas Customs." Diss. University of Illinois, 1937.

Johnson explores the influence of Greek and Roman traditions on Christmas, especially the holidays known as Saturnalia and the Kalends of January. Specific customs examined relate to food, mumming, role reversal, the Yule log, and greenery.

Johnson, Sheila K. "Christmas Card Syndrome." *New York Times Magazine* (5 December 1971), 38-39, 147-49, 151, 154, 158, 163.

This report is an adaptation of Johnson's earlier work (see below) in which she analyzes Christmas cards as indicators of social status and mobility aspirations. Social class has a greater impact than religious or ethnic ties on the sending of cards. Johnson discusses political, mimeographed, photo, and "dirty" cards.

————. "Sociology of Christmas Cards." *Trans-Action*, 8, no. 3 (January, 1971), 27-29.

Johnson discusses three types of sender-receiver relation-

ships; cards sent but not reciprocated; cards sent and
reciprocated; cards received but not reciprocated. Analysis
is mainly in terms of mobility aspirations and economics.
Johnson then turns to the cards themselves and discusses
how they reflect the sender's personality, interests, and
experiences.

Jones, Charles W. "Knickerbocker Santa Claus." *New-York*
    Historical Society Quarterly, 38 (1954), 357-85.

    Jones's article is one of the most frequently cited works
on the history of the Santa Claus figure in America. He
emphasizes the Dutch influence but also comments on the
effects of the writings of Washington Irving and Clement
Moore. Some researchers, especially de Groöt, dispute
Jones's assumptions that Santa Claus customs were introduced by seventeenth-century Dutch settlers. While the
Dutch brought some of their traditions to America, English
customs had an even stronger effect.

Jones, Ernest. "The Significance of Christmas" (1922). In
    his *Essays on Applied Psychoanalysis*, vol. 2. London:
    Hogarth, 1951, pp. 212-24.

    The essay begins with a discussion of the fixing of the
date of Christmas, noting that Christmas became more important with the increasing interest in Maryolatry.
Mythological origins, such as the boar's head representing
a totemic feast, are discussed. Jones briefly mentions
how Christmas came to be a children's festival incorporating
the psychological ideal of dissolving family discord in a
happy reunion. The paper becomes rather disjointed toward
the end, but it contains some interesting psychological
ideas.

Kane, Harnett T. *The Southern Christmas Book*. New York:
    David McKay, 1958.

    Although this is mainly a descriptive compilation, Kane
does present valuable information on the history and
development of Christmas observances in the southern
United States.

Kapros, Márta. "A karácsonyi kántalás formái és funkciói a
    dél-nyírségi." *Müvektség és Hagyomány*, 10 (1968), 219-
    30.

    Kapros studies a carol singing tradition and its functions
for three age groups: children (to receive presents),

youths (to meet girls), and adults (to reinforce good relations with members of the community).

Kaylor, Paul Evans. "Celebration: In Affirming the Celebra-
tive We Are Saying Yes! to Both What Is and What Can Be."
Mademoiselle, 72, no. 2 (December, 1970), 80-81.

Kaylor outlines the problems of Christmas celebrations
from both the religious and secular points of view. He
underscores the importance of festivity in man's total
environment. Christmas is both a Christian and a civic
observance and can be celebrated as a holy day and as a
cultural festival.

Kellner, K.A. Heinrich. *Heortologie, oder die geschichtliche
Entwicklung des Kirchenjahres und der Heiligenfeste von
den ältesten Zeiten bis zur Gegenwart.* Freiburg: Herder,
1901.

Christmas is included in this study of the cycle of
ecclesiastical festivals. Kellner looks at the process of
establishing the date of Christmas and then shifts to a
discussion of Christmas as a focus for other "festivals,"
such as Advent and Epiphany. Originally, Advent was considered a period of fasting and penance; later it became a
memorial period to the Old Testament, the time before
Christ. Epiphany was a Church festival before Christmas
was established. Its purpose was to honor the appearance
of the son of God, especially the times of his life in
which "His divine sonship was revealed in some distinctive
manner" (p. 166). Epiphany became a complex occasion to
mark the Nativity, the wise men's worship, Christ's baptism,
and the miracle at the marriage in Cana. With the appearance
of a specific date for Christ's Nativity, Epiphany lost
some of its character, but the Church continued to stress
its importance as the date of Christ's baptism when his
divinity became present to all.

Kemp, S.C. "Spaendingln mellem hedensk og kristen jul" ("The
Connection Between Pagan and Christian Christmas Celebrations"). *Kukens Verden*, n.v. (1968), 367-72.

King, Georgina G. "Shepherds and Kings." *Art and Archaeology*,
12 (1921), 265-72.

King's is an excellent work on the history of Nativity
scenes.

Kissling, Hermann. *Das Weihnachtsbild, ein Bildzyklus des Mittelalters.* Ratigen: A. Henn, 1972.

This is an art historical study of medieval paintings and illustrations depicting the Christmas story.

Klinger, Witold. *Obrzedowość ludowa Bożego Narodzenia, jej początek i zbaczenie pierwotne* (*The Folk-Ritual of Christmas*). Poznan: Fiszer i Majewski, 1926.

Koch, Georg. "Deutsche Weihnacht, eine volkskundliche Betrachtung." *Volk und Scholle,* 10 (1932), 319-24.

Köppen, Wilhelm. *Beiträge zur Geschichte der deutschen Weihnachtsspiele.* Paderborn: Ferdinand Schöningh, 1893.

Köppen surveys the history and development of Christmas dramas.

Koleva, T.A. "Zimnii tsikl obychaev yuzhnyx slavyan (k voprosu o strukturno-tipologicheskom analize obryadnosti)" ("The Winter Cycle of Customs among Southern Slavs (To the Problem of the Structural Typological Research into Customs)"). *Sovetskaja Etnografija,* n.v., no. 3 (May, 1971), 40-50.

The author applies the structural—typological method of comparative studies to the major components of Christmas and New Year rituals: Yule log, food, superstitions, songs, and mumming. The researcher seeks to understand the customs and rituals as a single whole and to trace their connection with other aspects of people's lives.

Krogman, Willy. "Die Wurzeln des Weihnachtsbaumes." *Rheinisches Jahrbuch für Volkskunde,* 13-14 (1962-1963), 60-80.

Krogman traces the Christmas tree's history back to Roman times. It was a means of warding off evil, a kind of magical life insurance for the coming year.

Kronfeld, Ernst Moritz. *Der Weihnachtsbaum, Botanik und Geschichte des Weihnachtsgrüns, seine Beziehungen zu Volksglauben Mythos, Kultur-Geschichte, Sage, Sitte und Dichtung.* Oldenburg and Leipzig: Schulzesche hof-Buchhandlung und hof Buchdruderei, n.d.

Kronfeld's thorough analysis of the history of the Christmas tree explores the roles played by the tree and tree symbolism in various cultures and religions. Then Kronfeld

looks at the various kinds of trees used--pine, fir--and
the growth of the custom's popularity in Alsace, Germany,
Austria, and other parts of the world.

Krumscheid, Alwin. "Humor in Weihnachtslied." *Kontakte*,
  6 (1967), 235-38.

German Christmas carols are almost all religious in
orientation but the author looks at some Spanish carols
with secular and humorous texts. Folk instruments and
noisemakers are also used in carol services where these
songs are performed.

Krythe, Mamie R. *All About American Holidays.* New York:
  Harper, 1962.

Krythe's work is a simple children's book (for ages 10-
13) but gives a good picture of the elements of Christmas
and their origins. Of particular interest is her discussion
of Nativity scenes.

————. *All About Christmas.* New York: Harper, 1954.

This book is directed to a popular audience. Krythe is
concerned with the history and development of many Christmas
customs and observances and artifacts, such as: Santa Claus,
greenery, trees, Nativity scenes, foods, candles, the star,
bells, cards, Christmas seals.

Kunz, Phillip R., and Michael Woolcott. "Season's Greetings:
  From My Status to Yours." *Social Science Research*, 5
  (1976), 269-78.

This is a report of an experiment in sending Christmas
cards to unknown professionals and blue-collar workers to
see if they would reciprocate despite not recognizing the
sender's name. Cards of varying quality, and indications
of the sender's status, were also used to see how they
would affect the response.

Kutter, Wilhelm. "Petzmärtle und Christkindle in oberen
  Enztal und verwandte Gestalten." In *Ländliche Kultur-
  formen im deutschen Südwestern. Festschrift für Heiner
  Heimburger*, ed. Peter Assion. Stuttgart: Kohlhammer,
  1971, pp. 203-15.

Kutter surveys the various types of southwestern German
Christmas gift-bringers: Petzmärtle, St. Nicholas, St.
Martin, the Christchild. He provides good background in-
formation on the historical and traditional relationships

between the figures but gives no reasons as to why a
specific figure should appear in one community and not in
another.

Lake, Kirsopp. "Christmas." *Hasting's Encyclopedia of
    Religion and Ethics*, vol. 3. New York: Scribners, 1908-
    27, pp. 601-8.

Lake explores the two main theories about the early
Catholic Church's decision on a day to celebrate Christmas.
He summarizes the work of two major scholars, Herman Usener
and L. Duchesne. Usener believed the celebration was
changed by Rome from January 6 to December 25 in A.D. 353
with January 6 remaining the Feast of Epiphany, the day of
Christ's baptism. Duchesne said that December 25 had
always been the Western date and January 6 was the Eastern
Church's holiday. Each group added the other's celebrations
to its initial observance. There is general agreement that
there is no evidence of a feast of the Nativity before the
fourth century except among a group known as the Basilidians,
who celebrated it on January 6 or on April 19 or 20. Lake
concludes that the Western Church's adoption of the December
date was motivated by a desire to draw attention from
heathen feasts held around the same time. He has a similar
article on Epiphany in vol. 5 of the *Hasting's Encyclopedia*,
pp. 330-32.

————. *The Christmas Festival*. New York: Privately printed,
    1937.

Lamas, Dubce Martins. *Pastorinhas Pastoris Présepios e
    Lapinhas*. Rio de Janeiro: Grafica Olimpica Editora
    LTDA, 1978.

Lamas's book is a not very successful, mainly descriptive
account of Brazilian shepherds plays with cursory socio-
cultural analysis.

Lassen, Hans. "Glaedelig Jul! Lidt om Julekortets Histoirie."
    Almanak, 69, no. 4 (1968), 33-36.

Lassen presents a brief examination of the history of
Christmas cards.

Latey, Maurice. "Give Us Back Our Christmas." *International
    Review*, 3 (1974), 55-58.

The author discusses the role of mythology and science
in shaping European attitudes toward Christianity and
Christmas from the seventeenth to the twentieth centuries.

Lauffer, Otto. "Noch einmal der Weihnachtsbaum." *Zeitschrift für Volkskunde*, 7 (1937), 60-64.

This is a brief historical study of the Christmas tree and its associated items, such as Christmas pyramids, Advent decorations, and ornaments.

Lebech, Modens. *Julemanden*. Copenhagen: Hassing, 1968.

This is an historical and comparative study of "Christmas men"--Santa Claus, St. Nicholas, the Scandinavian *Julenissen*-- covering their ecclesiastical origins and their friendly vs. pedagogical aspects in various countries (Denmark, England, and the United States).

Leclercq, J. "Aux origines du cycle de Noël." *Ephemerides Liturgicae*, 60 (1946), 7-26.

Leclercq's article is concerned with the development of the Christmas liturgy.

Leiber, Fritz. "Christmas Syndrome." *Science Digest*, 54, no. 6 (December, 1963), 16-21.

Leiber's article examines some of the sociological and psychological problems that result from celebrating Christmas in America. He notes four types of people who are susceptible to problems at Christmas: (1) the perennial child; (2) the neurotic overcompensator; (3) the status seeker; and (4) the tension prone. He offers some advice on how to cope with Christmas and preserve one's mental health.

Lemieux, Denise. "Le Temps et la fête dans la vie sociale." *Recherches Sociographiques*, 7 (1966), 281-304.

The festival is a privileged moment in man's existence, in some ways even resembling dreams. Lemieux examines the Christmas tree, the star, and other light symbols for their symbolic significance and history. She looks at the symbolic importance of snow in its association with the countryside, the true site of Christmas. She also seeks to explain some of the differences between ancient and modern Christmas celebrations and the contradictions of the spirit of the holiday inherent in modern society.

Lenz, Werner. *Alle Jahre Wieder, Weihnachten von A-Z*. Gütersloh: Bertel-mann Lexikon-Verlag, 1969.

Although this is a mainly descriptive work, it does contain some intriguing information on German attitudes toward

such American Christmas customs as egg nog, special postage
stamps, and Santa Claus.

Léon-Portilla, Miguel. "Cantos de Navidad en lengua náhuatl."
    In 25 estudios de folklore. Homenaje a Vicente T. Mendoza
    y Virginia Rodriguez Rivera. Mexico City: Universidad
    Nacional Autónoma de Mexico, Instituto de Investigaciones
    Estéticas, 1971, pp. 167-70.

Christmas in the New World dates from the efforts of early
Franciscan missionaries. Conquered Indians were quick to
assimilate new cultural elements, such as Christmas customs.

Lévi-Strauss, Claude. "Le Père Noël supplicié." Les Temps
    Modernes, 7 (1952), 1572-90.

This fascinating article was prompted by some ecclesiastical pronouncements in 1951 that the French traditional
figure of Père Noël should be abolished. Lévi-Strauss
reviews the use of Christmas before World War II and afterwards, the effect of American Christmas customs (through
stimulus diffusion rather than direct influence), and the
periods of popularity and disfavor in the history of
Christmas. He discusses Père Noël's characteristics; he
is kindly, used in an educative and primitive manner, and
is a symbol of the differences and exchanges between the
upper (adult) and lower (children, poor) classes. He makes
some interesting statements about the relationships between
death, children, and initiations, e.g., that Christmas is
a "dead" time of year (winter), children are dead (un-
initiated), and Christmas is a children's festival (as are
many autumn festivals from Halloween onward).

————. "Where Does Father Christmas Come From?" New Society,
    2, no. 64 (19 December 1963), 6-8.

In this rather abstract article Father Christmas is portrayed as a symbol of the benevolent authority of elders who
also expresses differences in status between children and
adults. He is also an illusion whose revelation is a rite
of passage. Lévi-Strauss also states that autumn is a
season of the progressive recognition of the return of the
dead, culminating with Christmas when the dead receive
presents (e.g., in the Scandinavian custom of leaving
dishes of food out) and then disappear until the next year.
Father Christmas is one of the representatives of the differences between the dead and the living; he leaves evidence
of his "existence" but is never really seen. He is also
the heir and antithesis of the medieval Abbot of Unreason
and an improvement in our relations with death.

Levy, Florence J. "On the Significance of Christmas for the 'Wolf Man.'" *Psychoanalytic Review*, 55 (1968-1969), 615-22.

Levy explores the impact of Christmas customs on the mental health of a particular psychiatric patient.

Lewy, Immanuel. "From Santa Claus to Santa Stooge." *Life*, 21, no. 25 (17 December 1951), 32-33.

This photographic essay depicts various Santas—in Texan garb, arriving via a helicopter, and appearing on a submarine.

Lid, Nils. *Joleband og Vegetasjons-Guddorn*. Oslo: I Komision hos J. Dybwad, 1928.

Lid analyzes Christmas as a kind of harvest festival, with particular attention to customs which show connections with gods and spirits of vegetation, such as Christmas cakes and Christmas trees.

————. "Jolesveinar og Groderikdomsgudar." *Skrifter utg av det Norske Urdens Kapsakademi*, 3 (1932), 1-175.

Lid discusses fertility symbols found in Christmas customs and also associated with pagan Nordic gods.

————. "Um Upphavet til Jolehogtidi." *Syn og Segn*, 31 (1925), 417-34.

This is another essay on the origin of the Christmas festival.

Liman, Ingemar. *Julens ABC. En Bok om Vara Jultraditioner*. Stockholm: Forum, 1971.

Liman's work is a standard historical/descriptive presentation.

Lincoln, Rabbi David H. "Christmas, the Rabbi Spoke Early: What It's Like to Be Jewish at Christmastime." *PTA Magazine*, 68, no. 4 (December, 1973), 22-25.

Rabbi Lincoln does not feel that public Christmas displays affect the Judaism of Jews. Jews who are marginal are more apt to be affected.

Lueschen, Guenther, et al. "Family Organization, Interaction and Ritual." *Journal of Marriage and the Family*, 33 (1971), 228-34.

The investigators use Christmas rituals as one test of
their hypothesis that family rituals will develop to
stabilize family and kinship relationships in modern societies. It is also judged that Christmas is more important
in modern societal settings than in traditional ones.
Christmas is not richer, but specific patterns of celebration are more differentiated and more functional in activating
family members.

—————. "Family, Ritual and Secularization: A Cross-National
    Study Conducted in Bulgaria, Finland, Germany and Ireland."
    Social Compass, 16 (1972), 519-36.

The researchers studied the adjustments of family and
kinship systems to modernizing influences. With the lessen-
ing of the influence of organized religion, Christmas became
oriented more to family celebrations and intra-family
visiting. Interest in sacred (or religious) aspects has
not disappeared but has become more private. This article
is an outstanding example of the recent work done on the
secularization of Christmas, especially in that it examines
four different types of secularization: (1) desacralization
with rationalization; (2) freedom from organized control of
religion; (3) "denaturing" of religious values into secular
ones; and (4) loss of significance of religious thinking
and institutions.

McArthur, A. Allan. *The Evolution of the Christian Year*.
    London: SCM Press, 1953.

McArthur looks at the history of and contrasts between
Christmas and Epiphany in the Eastern and Western Catholic
Churches. He also explores the relationship between Roman
mid-winter festivals, the festival of the Invincible Sun
(Natalis Solis Invicti), and the early Catholic Church's
commemorations of the Incarnation.

McCurdy, Robert M., and Edith M. Coulter. *A Bibliography of
    Articles Relating to Holidays*. Boston: Boston Book Co.,
    1907.

The bibliography lists a good selection of historical/
descriptive articles on Christmas customs, literature,
and celebrations around the world.

MacGregor-Villareal, Mary. "Celebrating *Las Posadas* in Los
    Angeles." *Western Folklore*, 39 (1980), 71-105.

This is an excellent, multi-faceted discussion of an
Hispanic Christmas celebration. MacGregor-Villareal

describes and analyzes four *las posadas* presentations.
Celebrations are presented for historical/cultural reasons,
as well as economic and religious ones. Home presentations
of *las posadas* are models for public ones but are not sup-
planted by the larger celebrations. Differences between
public and private celebrations are examined, such as the
distinction between performers and observers, the expansion
of social elements, the increased display of ethnicity,
and the concern with authenticity. Public *posadas* succeed
because of their distinctive traits, theatrical nature, and
planned, organized entertainment.

McKnight, George Harley. *St. Nicholas, His Legend and His
Role in the Christmas Celebrations and Other Popular
Customs.* New York: Putnam, 1917; rpt. Williamstown,
Mass.: Corner House, 1974.

McKnight investigates the history, both actual and
legendary, of the figures of St. Nicholas, Santa Claus,
and Kris Kringle. McKnight also looks at St. Nicholas's
status as a patron saint, especially that of schoolboys
and dowerless maidens. Examples of dramas surrounding the
figure are examined. Stress is placed on St. Nicholas's
humanness and kindness and how this has influenced the
customs involving him.

Mak, Jacobus Johannes. *Het Kerstfest, Ontstaan in Verbreiding,
Viering in de Middeleeuwen.* 'S-Gravenhage: Martinus
Nijhoff, 1948.

The first part of Mak's book examines the general development of Epiphany and Christmas, both the Christian and pagan
components. The second part covers specific symbols and
customs (with an emphasis on light and Nativity scenes)
and the various days of the season: Christmas Eve, St.
Stephen's Day, and New Year's, as well as Christmas and
Epiphany. Christian associations and relationships to
pagan festivals are both addressed.

————. *Middeleeuwse Kerst Voorstellingen.* Utrecht and
Brussels: Uitgeverij het Spectrum, 1948.

This is an extensive examination of the artistic and
iconographic aspects of Christmas, especially as portrayed
in Nativity scenes.

Maleš, Branimiro. "Apuntes sobre Navidad y Año Nuevo."
Revista de Antropología y Ciencias Afines, 1 (1952-1953),
53-71.

While concentrating on Christmas and New Year's customs
in Serbia, Maleš also presents a comparative study of various
peoples' conceptions of the annual "rebirth" of the sun.

Maller, Allen S. "Hanukkah Is Not Jewish Christmas." *US
    Catholic*, 38 (December, 1973), 28-29.

Although Hanukkah may be more important now because it
is attempting to compete with Christmas, it is also more
relevant to Jews as a symbol of national liberation.

Manga, János. "Szlovák kapcsolatok a palóc karácsonyi
    szokásokban." *Ethnographia*, 59 (1948), 94-102.

Manga's study is concerned with the influence of Christianity and Slavic customs on Hungarian Christmas celebrations.

Mannhardt, Wilhelm. *Weihnachtsblüthen in Sitte und Sage.*
    Berlin: F. Duncker, 1864.

The first part of Mannhardt's book deals with stories
about Jesus' childhood. The second is concerned with the
history of Christmas and its celebrations, legends, and
customs, such as religious plays and the Magi.

Marbach, Johannes. *Die Heilige Weihnachtszeit. Nach Bedeutung
    Geschichte, Sitten und Symbolen.* Frankfurt: J.D. Sauer-
    länder, 1865.

This historical/developmental assessment of Christmas
begins with a look at pagan views of nature as manifested
in winter festivals. The Christian origins of the holiday
are then analyzed: the birth of Christmas, the early significance of Epiphany, the migration of customs to a
separate Christmas festival. The conflict surrounding
the syncretization of pagan and Christian symbols and observances is thoroughly explored here, in contrast to many
works which skim over the problem in order to present an
idyllic concept of the associations between pagan and
Christian, insofar as a holiday such as Christmas is concerned.

Margetson, S. "Medieval Nativity Plays." *History Today*,
    22 (1972), 850-57.

The author is mainly concerned with the history of
Nativity plays, but she does provide some analysis. The
story of Christ's birth was acted out in the vernacular so
that people could better understand its message of joy and

salvation. The plays made people aware that the vulgar
instincts of man could be redeemed by divine intervention;
they were also an attempt to humanize Christianity. In
addition, they served to illustrate the contrast between
sacred and secular.

Marti-Ibeñez, Felix. "On Christmas and Neurosis: An Editorial
    Introduction." In *Psychiatry and Religion*, ed. Werner
    Wolff. New York: MD Publications, 1955, pp. 57-62.

Marti-Ibeñez believes that some personal conflicts are
intensified via unconscious connections with religious
mysteries. Many neuroses are related to special hours,
days, months, and seasons. December 25 was originally the
time for a feast celebrating the return of the sun, upon
which life depended. Man was afraid that his sins would
prevent its return. In some neuroses the rituals surrounding sin and punishment, rebirth and salvation, are
enacted through the depression and hypomaniacal excitement
surrounding New Year's.

Matz, Milton. "The Meaning of the Christmas Tree to the
    American Jew." *Jewish Journal of Sociology*, 3 (1961),
    129-37.

Matz's study involves second- and third-generation Reform
Jews. Second-generation Jews are often against having a
tree; they still see it as a religious affront. A third-
generation Jew has secularized the tree and adopts it because it affirms his position as an American, yet he still
admires the Jew who does not feel the need for a tree.
Matz concludes that a child may need a Christmas tree to
"hyphenate his Jewish ethnicism."

Mead, Margaret. "Can Christmas Bring the Generations To-
    gether." *Redbook*, 142, no. 2 (December, 1973), 27-28.

Mead's editorial discusses the problems recently married
couples (or new parents) have in relation to Christmas
celebrations; should they celebrate as their parents did,
or devise new customs, or go away for the holidays. Mead
suggests certain compromises, but suggests that the couple
first sit down and decide which rituals are really important to keep and which can be modified or adapted.

Meerloo, Joost Abraham Maurits. "Santa Claus and the Psychol-
    ogy of Giving." *American Practitioner*, 11 (1960), 1031-
    35.

After the Reformation, the Protestant countries continued

to believe in one Catholic saint, St. Nicholas. He appealed
to unconscious needs to give and procreate. Meerloo
believes most people have a great deal of trouble giving
freely, without any thought of return. A gift makes one
feel obliged to return immediately one of equal value to
"neutralize magically the intention of the giver" (p. 1033).
The author proposes four main patterns of giving: (1) magic
giving (to take possession of the environment); (2) gifts
as bribes (to be the omnipotent provider); (3) mechanization
of giving (giving money); and (4) mature giving.

Mennesson-Rigaud, Odette. "Noël Voodou en Haiti." *Présence-
Africaine*, no. 12 (1951), 37–60.

Meyer, Arnold. *Das Weihnachtsfest. Seine Entstehung und
Entwicklung.* Tübingen: J.C.B. Mohr, 1913.

Meyer is interested in both ecclesiastical and lay
Christmases. Regarding the former he discusses the influence of Gnostic and Dionysian cults and the fixing of the
date of Christ's birth. On the lay side he discusses folk
customs, Nativity scenes, and gift-bringers.

Miles, Clement A. *Christmas in Ritual and Tradition, Christian and Pagan.* London and Leipzig: T. Fischer Unwin,
1912.

This thorough and well-written book is basically historical but offers some insight into the reasons behind
the celebration of Christmas and the use of its elements.
Miles is mainly interested in origins and combines a great
many theories and approaches, although his own personal
preference is for ritualistic and survivalistic theories.
He comments on the influence of modern civilization and
Protestantism on the Christmas celebration and also notes
that the keeping of Christmas reflects national character,
the germ of an idea that is not further developed until
Barnett's discussion more than forty years later.

Miller, E.F. "Contradictions of Christmas." *Ligourian*, 57
(December, 1969), 2–4.

Miller gives a good presentation of Christmas's opposi-
tions—sacred and secular, giving and getting, loneliness
and reunion—but with a heavy theological interpretation.

Miller, Heather R. "The Candlewalk: A Midwinter Fire Festival." *North Carolina Folklore*, 19 (1971), 153–56.

The Candlewalk is held on Christmas Eve and New Year's
Eve in parts of the American South. It is closed to whites
and "non-believers." The Candlewalk includes a withdrawal
of black females into a forest (symbolizing sexual indoctrination), "fertility" rites, and an adoration of Mary and
Jesus. A fire, made both in celebration and out of fear,
symbolizes the return of the sun. It is also a purification
mechanism which is necessary because of the evils of
modern technology. Miller analyzes the Candlewalk in terms
of survivals theory, drawing heavily upon Frazerian ideas.

Monks, James L. *Great Catholic Festivals.* New York: Henry
Schuman, Inc., 1951.

Monks includes a very brief section on Christmas in
which he discusses the origin of the celebration, the
process of establishing the date, and early Christmas
dramas.

Montero, A. "Misterio y folklore de la Navidad." *Studium*,
9 (1965), 503-17.

The mystery of Christmas is considered in the light of
numerous biblical passages. Spiritual implications for
individual Christians are developed. The question of the
actual date of Jesus' birth is raised, and various customs
are described.

Montgomery, John Warwick. "Remythologizing Christmas."
Christianity Today, 13 (1968), 251-54.

This theological essay compares the Christmas story to
other myths and legends, such as Sleeping Beauty. Then
follows a symbolical analysis of traditional elements:
the tree, family reunions, dinners, and Santa Claus.

Monthan, Guy, and Doris Monthan. *Nacimientos. Nativity
Scenes by Southwest Indian Artisans.* Flagstaff, Ariz.:
Northland Press, 1979.

The introduction to this book provides a history of the
development of Nativity scenes among the various Indian
groups of the southwestern United States. The bulk of
the volume is a beautiful compilation of photographs of
Nativity scenes from the region with information on the
context of their creation.

Montmorency, J.E.G. de. "Christmas Mummers." *Contemporary
    Review*, 103 (1913), 129-34.

    The author gives a brief history of Christmas mumming
practices.

Moos, Hermann. "Vom Ursprung und Sinn des Weihnachtsschenkens,
    Um einen alten Kultvers." *Unsere Heimat*, n.v. (1938-
    1939), 66-68.

    This article is concerned with the origins and meaning of
giving gifts at Christmas.

Moschetti, Gregory J. "Christmas Potlatch: A Refinement on
    the Sociological Interpretation of Gift Exchange."
    Sociological Focus, 12 (1979), 1-7.

    Moschetti's abstract for this article reads: "This paper
examines certain asymmetries in the Christmas gift exchange
such that one class of persons receives more than is given.
The classic case is that of children, vis-a-vis parents,
but other instances can be found. These asymmetries are
examined in terms of their symbolic significance. That is,
they are seen to reflect differential dependencies of constituent bodies on the collectivity and each one's authority
to act as its agent."

Mottinger, Alvina H. "Stories of Favorite Christmas Carols."
    Musician, Journal of Musical History, 3, no. 3 (1965),
    33-48.

    The texts and brief histories of fourteen Christmas
carols are provided.

Muir, Frank. *Christmas Customs and Traditions*. London:
    Sphere Books, 1975.

    Muir's book is a basic historical/descriptive effort.
He discusses the establishment of the date of Christmas,
pagan origins, and various customs, and includes poetry,
dramatic scenes, and art to illustrate his points. His
work is extensive in scope but cursory in analysis, and
rather amusing as he occasionally injects some personal
notes.

Müller, Gerhard. *Weihnacht der Deutschen, aus Geschichte und
    Brauchtum in der Weihnachtszeit*. Karlsruhe: Badenia-
    Verlag, 1946.

    Müller finds the origin of the Christmas festival in
birthday celebrations for ancient pagan gods. His historical

coverage of ecclesiastical and folk practices includes
Advent (St. Barbara's Day, St. Thomas's Day, St. Nicholas's
Day), Christmas trees, Nativity scenes, songs, art, plays,
food, St. Stephen's Day, St. John's Day, New Year's Eve,
New Year's, and Epiphany.

Murdock, Richard E. "A Family Festival Cluster." *Religious
Education*, 72 (1977), 528-33.

It is often on winter holidays that secularism and family
dysfunction can first be noted. Each family has its own
festival clusters of rituals which affirm the values of
the holiday and relate biblical themes to the family's
members.

Myers, Robert J. *Celebrations, the Complete Book of American
Holidays*. Garden City, N.Y.: Doubleday, 1972.

In this historical/descriptive work, Myers briefly
touches on many areas but does present a great deal of
information. He discusses the influence of Mithraism on
early Christmas celebrations, as well as the effects of
Saturnalia and the later Puritan repression of the holiday.
Other items of focus are the development of Christmas in
the New World, Santa Claus, carols, Gian Carlo Menotti's
opera "Amahl and the Night Visitors," the Yule log, candles
and electric lights, cards, food, greenery, mumming, and
superstitions.

Nettel, Reginald, ed. *Carols, 1400-1950: A Book of Christmas
Carols*. Bedford, England: Gordon Fraser, 1956.

The introduction contains a good history of Christmas
carols and carolling. It is expanded in his later book
(see below).

————. *Christmas and Its Carols*. London: Faith Press,
1960.

This book contains perceptive comments on the nature and
function of Christmas carols (e.g., their portrayal of
men's and women's roles; the influence of "pop" songs and
television), but it is basically historically oriented.
The dance origins of carols and their relationships with
ballads and hymns are discussed, as well as their being
representatives of fertility lore. Songs associated with
Nativity scenes and miracle plays are surveyed, as are
the origins and purposes of wassailing, the changes in
Christmas because of the Puritans, Dickens and the influence
of the nineteenth century, and carols in the United States.

Nettl, Paul. "O Tannenbaum." *American-German Review*, 15,
no. 8 (December, 1948), 6-7, 9.

Nettl reviews the history of the Christmas tree and its
associated song "O Tannenbaum."

Neuhoff, Dorothy A. "Christmas in Colonial America." *Social
Studies*, 40 (1949), 339-49.

Neuhoff discusses different types of colonial celebra-
tions and their incorporation with each other, which re-
sulted in a uniquely American Christmas. She includes the
Puritans, the Dutch and English in New York, the Anglicans
in Virginia, the French in Louisiana, and the Catholics in
South America. She also provides some information on the
Christmases of Indians who had come into contact with
Jesuit missionaries.

Newberry, Wilma. "The Solstitial Holidays in Carmen Laforet's
Nada: Christmas and Midsummer." *Romance Notes*, 17 (1976),
76-78.

This is a good analysis of the Christmas theme in literature; it emphasizes characters' disorientation because of
the opposition between the reality of their lives and the
significance of Christmas.

Nilsson, M.P. "At Which Time of the Year Was the Pre-
Christian Yule Celebrated." *ARV*, 14 (1958-1959), 108-14.

Nilsson uses linguistic evidence to answer his question.

————. "Studien zur Vorgeschichte des Weihnachtsfestes."
Archiv für Religionswissenschaft, 19 (1916-1919), 50-150.

This is a lengthy survey of the pagan feasts which evolved
into Christmas, such as the Kalends of January, Saturnalia,
and Compitali. He traces the origins of Christmas to
Babylonian-Persian festivals and discusses the influence
of both Roman and Germanic customs.

Nitzsche, G.E. *The Christmas Putz of the Pennsylvania Germans.*
Publications of the Pennsylvania German Folklore Society,
vol. 6. Kutztown, Pa.: Pennsylvania German Folklore
Society, 1941, pp. 1-28.

The *putz* is an elaborate Nativity scene, often including
landscapes and sometimes covering an entire room. Nitzsche
insists that his main intention is to prove that the *putz*
is limited to Pennsylvania Germans, but he makes comparisons

with Spanish and Latin American scenes and also with the French *crèche* and Germanic *krippe*.

Nosova, G.A. "Osyt Etnografichesheskogo Izucheniya Bytovogo Pravoslaviya Materialakh" ("A Preliminary Ethnographic Study of Habitual Orthodoxy"). *Problems of Scientific Atheism*, no. 3 (1967), 151-63 (in Russian).

A 1965 study of a Russian village revealed that religious calendrical feasts were still observed and that magical rituals, such as chalk on the door at Epiphany, also exist. The remaining vestiges of religious ritual have a tendency toward loss of religious content.

Ohlson, Ella. "Julskröcka. En isolerad tradition och dess upplösning." *Angermanland-Medelpad*, n.v. (1933), 138-51.

Ohlson's article investigates the custom of giving children switches at Christmas.

Onasch, Konrad. *Das Weihnachtsfest im orthodoxen Kirchenjahr, Liturgie und Ikonographie*. Berlin: Evangelische Verlags-anstalt, 1958.

This book, heavily theologically oriented, explores the origins of Christmas in Eastern Orthodox celebrations, the place of Christmas in the ecclesiastical year, its relationship to Pentecost, Easter, and Epiphany, and the process of fixing the date of Christ's birth. Some forms of Christmas iconography are discussed also.

Oswalt, Wendell H. "A Particular Pattern: Santa Claus." In his *Understanding Our Culture: An Anthropological View*. New York: Holt, Rinehart and Winston, 1970, pp. 6-11.

Oswalt provides a brief history of St. Nicholas and Santa Claus, then details Santa's emerging popularity in the United States. His magical appearance is a psychologically satisfying alternative to real-life competition. Rather cursory comments are made on the shift from the sacred religious personality of St. Nicholas to the secular folk hero of Santa Claus, which was accomplished without a drastic change in physical form. However, Oswalt considers only a few of the many depictions of St. Nicholas and the evolving Santa Claus.

Palmer, Geoffrey, and Noel Lloyd. *A Year of Festivals: A Guide to British Calendar Customs*. London: Frederick Warne, 1972.

Here is another historical/descriptive book covering pagan origins, Christmas in the Middle Ages, the effect of Cromwell, mumming, carols, Father Christmas and Santa Claus, evergreens, trees, and cards.

Parker, Karla V. "Festival of the Child." *National Parent-Teacher*, 55, no. 4 (December, 1960), 3.

Commercialization is the material symbol of man's wish to respond to the spiritual symbols of Christmas. At the center of the holiday is the child. Christmas celebrates birth and creation, and the child thus becomes the most important creature on earth. The beauty of Christmas is not abstract or general but personal and specific.

Paru, Marden D. "Tannenbaum and the Jewish Problem." *Jewish Social Studies*, 35 (1973), 283-89.

Paru discusses the problems Jews have with Christmas symbols (their adoption and fear of assimilation) and corresponding magnification of Hanukkah. Since the 1950s, Hanukkah has been influenced by events in Israel and has thus become more important. Paru presents and tests a hypothesis about the type of Jew who has a Christmas tree. S/he is likely to be ambivalent about his/her Jewishness, more assimilated into American culture, less observant of traditional Jewish rituals, and a young parent of children under seventeen.

Pask, Arthur T. "Evolution of Christmas Annuals." *Windsor Magazine*, 2 (1895), 697-709.

This wide-ranging and thorough history of news supplements and small books ("annuals") published in England at Christmastime suggests that their origins lie in Dickens's *A Christmas Carol*, which was originally published in small keepsake form.

Pearce, T.M. "The New Mexican Shepherds' Play." *Western Folklore*, 15 (1956), 77-88.

Los Pastores are Christmas plays based on the birth of Christ which are often performed in Catholic churches. Pearce traces their history in the Southwest United States, mainly through texts. He delineates twelve main episodes, including *las posadas* (see citation for Mary MacGregor-Villareal), the song of the star, and the adorations and offerings.

Pearson, Norah F. *The Stories of Our Christmas Customs*. Loughborough, England: Wills and Hepworth, 1964.

This children's book covers the history of Christmas Day, especially early ecclesiastical observances and the Puritan influence. Pearson stresses the importance of light, heat, and candles in various customs and also discusses Nativity scenes and plays, carols, greenery, trees, ornaments and decorations, gifts, cards, pantomimes, food, and Santa Claus.

Petersen, William J. "Postcard Holiday Greetings." *Palimpsest*, 48 (1967), 569-84.

This short, cursory article includes many illustrations. The emphasis is on the history of holiday postcards with some rarely cited data on their development in America.

Petneki, Anna. "Die polnischen Koleda-Lieder im Mittelalter." *Studia Musicol*, 15 (1973), 165-73.

Petneki discusses the historical and musical relationships between secular and sacred forms of the Polish *koleda*, a type of Christmas song.

Pigot, George. *A Vindication of the Practice of the Ancient Church as Well as the Church of England and Other Reformed Churches, in the Observation of Christmas Day*. Boston: T. Fleet, 1731.

One of the earliest assessments of Christmas, this book attacks the Puritan repression of Christmas.

Pimlott, J.A.R. "Arts in Society: Christmas Pops." *New Society*, 2, no. 64 (19 December 1963), 25.

Pimlott reviews the carol-singing tradition, especially in the nineteenth and twentieth centuries. He chooses the top twelve Christmas songs in England and looks at their common features. All were composed before 1900, so he stresses how Christmas looks backward, is extremely traditional, and does not like innovation.

————. "... But Once a Year." *New Society*, 1, no. 12 (20 December 1962), 9-12.

Pimlott is interested in the compulsive nature of participation in the Christmas celebration. He divides participation into four types: religious; holiday from work; the "orgy" (various excesses); and the concern for others

which emphasizes social cohesion. Social harmony and the
spirit of good will are strongest within the family but
there is a looking outward to friends, neighbors, workmates,
and the community at large.

————. *The Englishman's Christmas: A Social History.*
Hassocks: Harvester Press, 1978.

The author traces the development of Christmas as a social
institution. It was popular in medieval and Tudor England,
then attacked by the Puritans and "abolished" in 1652, but
new Christmas charities were founded and mummers plays continued to be produced. Christmas was revitalized during
the Victorian period due to the influence of Prince Albert
and Charles Dickens. Specific items of investigation are
trees, cards, Father Christmas, food, and Nativity plays.

————. "Merry Christmas." *History To-Day*, 3 (1953), 853-
60.

This historical survey of Christmas in England covers
the pagan origins of the Yule log, the lack of impact of
some continental customs (such as the Feast of Fools), the
effects of the Reformation, and nineteenth-century revitaliza-
tion.

Pischel, Barbara. "Preussisch-Friedland und seine Parzen."
Jahrbuch für Volkskunde der Heimatvertribenen, 6 (1961),
147-82.

Pischel gives a detailed description of services celebrated
on Christmas in Protestant Polish churches.

Plath, David W. "The Japanese Popular Christmas: Coping with
Modernity." *Journal of American Folklore*, 76 (1963),
309-17.

To the Japanese, Christmas is part of the modern lifestyle, a part of what can make modernity meaningful. Plath
traces the development of Christmas in Japan from its
beginnings in the sixteenth century to its boom in the
1800s to its present acceptance. It is not interpreted as
a religious threat by other Japanese religions, especially
since it does not interfere with their New Year's celebrations. Christmas is considered democratic and American in
its emphasis on materialism. Santa Claus is an important
element; he has some connections with other traditional
Japanese figures, is not considered a moral arbiter, and
has been accepted more by the Japanese than by other non-
Western groups observing Christmas.

————. "Overworked Japan and the Holiday Demiurge." *Today's Japan (Orient West)*, 5 (August, 1960), 61-64.

Poston, Elizabeth. *The Second Penguin Book of Christmas Carols*. Harmondsworth, Middlesex, and Baltimore: Penguin Books, 1970.

Poston uses predominantly American sources. She gives text, music, and notes on the history of each carol.

Poulaille, Henry. *La Grande et Belle Bible des Noëls anciens du XII-XVI siècle*, 3 vols. Paris: A. Michel, 1942-1951.

Poulaille has produced an extensive collection and study of songs and poetry associated with the history of Christmas. He looks at Christmas celebrations in the Church and theatre, mystery plays, and Christmas art.

Prentice, N.M.; Martin Manosevitz; and Laura Hubbs. "Imaginary Figures of Childhood: Santa Claus, Easter Bunny, and the Tooth Fairy." *American Journal of Orthopsychiatry*, 48 (1978), 618-28.

The investigators' research involves the developmental progression of children's beliefs as revealed through structured interviewing and parents' questionnaires. Belief in imaginary figures varied with a child's age and level of parental encouragement. Belief in the three figures is unrelated to other indices of children's fantasy involvement.

Prentice, N.M.; L.K. Schmechel; and M. Manosevitz. "Children's Belief in Santa Claus, Developmental Study of Fantasy and Causality." *Journal of the American Academy of Child Psychiatry*, 18 (1979), 658-67.

Belief in Santa Claus declines with age and as causal reasoning increases. Age seven is the transitional time as the child becomes adventurous about his/her belief in Santa Claus. Some children retain belief longer than others in spite of their perception of logical inconsistencies because there are incentives to continue believing.

Proctor, James T. "Children's Reactions to Christmas." *Journal of the Oklahoma State Medical Association*, 60 (1967), 653-59.

Proctor begins with a brief discussion of the history and evolution of Christmas. He then moves to a discussion of children's reactions to Santa Claus (which Proctor considers equivalent to their reactions to Christmas as a

whole). Children's expectations differ with maturity and
psychological development. He also reviews other psychological works on Christmas by Sereno, Sterba, Jekels, Jones,
Boyer, Eisenbud, and Catell.

Raglan, Lord. "The Riddle of the Magi." *New Society*, 2, no.
    65 (26 December 1963), 9-10.

The author discusses the appearance of the story of the
Magi in the narratives of many ancient cultures.

Rasband, Ester. *What Think You of Christmas.* Salt Lake
    City, Utah: Bookcroft, 1978.

Reid, Ira. "The John Canoe Festival." *Phylon*, 3 (1942),
    349-70.

Reid's article is a simple review of this Black festival
which occurs at Christmastime.

Reid, Robert Ewen. "Infantile Crises Associated with Christ-
    mas. (A Psychoanalytic Interpretation)." Diss. School
    of Theology, Claremont, Ca., 1968.

Reid's work is an attempt to clarify the infantile beginnings of psychological processes through an understanding
of the content of Christmas. He pays particular attention
to Santa Claus's being/non-being polarity, the holiday's
pagan origins, its symbolism of death and rebirth, and the
coming of light. He believes its celebration of birth
intensifies death anxiety which leads to negative feelings.
Christmas confronts memories from infancy and early childhood which produces the stress, depression, and hostility
often encountered at Christmas. Reid then discusses the
dynamics of the oral stage (trust versus mistrust) and the
"virtue of Hope." The latter is the critical dimension of
Christmas.

Ribeyrol, Monette. "Fêtes traditionelles et fêtes nouvelles
    en Bulgarie socialiste." *Ethnopsychologie*, 28 (1973),
    441-59.

The author's research has concluded that contemporary
Bulgarian celebrations devoted to family, work, and the
nation have been maintained, while those dealing with
religion, although not prohibited, are not popular. They
do remain outside of state control.

Richard, Wolfram. "Weihnachtsgast und 'Heiliges Mah.'" *Zeitschrift für Volkskunde*, 58 (1962), 1-31.

Richard discusses the German peasant custom of welcoming poor or transient guests at a Christmas holiday feast. Offerings of food from the table are made to plants, fields, and animals as a survival of an ancient mid-winter life-renewal ritual related to the time when Woden, who was considered a guest, ruled over life and death.

Richards, Katherine Lambert. *How Christmas Came to the Sunday-Schools*. New York: Dodd, Mead, and Co., 1934.

This is one of the basic historical works on Christmas. Richards discusses pagan elements and the effect of the Reformation, Christmas in the American colonies, the appearance, development, and acceptance of Christmas activities in American Sunday Schools, and the political and social influences which made this acceptance favorable. At first, Sunday Schools ignored Christmas, but ideas changed after the Civil War. Christmas became popular because people wanted something special; the joy and beauty of the holiday appealed to their usually somber lifestyle. It gave tangible form to ideas and emotions. The Sunday School celebrations are likened to the decorating of medieval churches and represent an interplay between secular and religious forces. They encourage gifts to the needy and promote world peace, with children being expected to play an active part.

Riddlehough, Geoffrey B. "Bad Will Towards Men: Ill-Tempered Christmas Carols." *Queen's Quarterly*, 54 (1947), 500-6.

In many pre-nineteenth-century English and French Christmas carols resentful verses were directed toward biblical figures (Adam, Herod) and toward Jews, Huguenots, contemporary inhabitants of neighboring districts, Cromwell, the Roundheads, and the Puritans. In the nineteenth century the carol was "tamed" as animosity was considered bad form at Christmastime; however, a few barbed songs still persist.

Riemerschmidt, Ulrich. *Weihnachten, Kult und Brauch, Einst und Jetzt*. Hamburg: Marion von Schröder, 1962.

In a rather moralistic fashion the author surveys the development of popular and folk Christmas celebrations, St. Nicholas, Nativity scenes and plays, food, and Christmas cards. The emphasis is on Germany but other areas are mentioned.

Rietschel, George. *Weihnachten in Kirche, Kunst und Volks-leben*. Leipzig: Veihagen and Klasing, 1902.

Rietschel surveys the portrayal of the Nativity of Christ in sculpture, painting, and Nativity scenes.

Ristow, W.W. "Worlds of Christmas Greetings." *Quarterly Journal of the Library of Congress*, 35 (1978), 234-41.

This mainly descriptive article concentrates on Christmas cards with maps.

Robbins, W.L. "Christmas Shooting Rounds in America and Their Backgrounds." *Journal of American Folklore*, 86 (1973), 48-52.

Robbins discusses the origins and parallels with European practices of an American Christmas custom. Rifles are shot off in some parts of the country to wish people a good year.

Roberts, L. "Reflections on the Christmas Spirit." *Harper's*, 170 (December, 1934), 117-21.

The author contributes a lay analysis of the impact of commercialization (note the date) and the desire for a simpler, more meaningful Christmas.

Rodgers, Edith Cooperrider. *Discussions of Holidays in the Later Middle Ages*. New York: Columbia University Press, 1940.

There is some mention of Christmas in her discussion of the observances of ecclesiastical feasts and holy days.

Roodin, Paul A.; Glen M. Vaught; and William E. Simpson. "Christmas Tree Drawings Before and After Christmas." *Perceptual Motor Skills*, 33 (1971), 365-66.

Here is another contribution to the literature on "naturally motivated expectancies." Assumptions of such tests include: (1) the symbol is important to the holiday; (2) changes in drawings reflect changes in motivation perceptions; (3) size of drawings increases as the holiday approaches and decreases afterwards; (4) a monotonic relationship exists between perceptions and motives in the drawings. Subjects were asked to make drawings of Christmas trees and coffee cups before and after Christmas. The width of the Christmas trees increased as Christmas approached. The coffee cups became more embellished, probably as a result of repeated testing.

Rothchild, Sylvia. "Christmas in Suburbia." *Hadassah News-letter*, 46 (December, 1964), 11, 16.

Rothchild gives a sensitive account of a suburban New York community's crises over the observance of Christmas in public schools. More than a mere description, the article comments on the various attitudes—legal, social, emotional—held by the various segments of the community.

Ruland, Josef, ed. *Weihnachten in Deutschland*. Bonn and Bad Godesberg: Hohwacht, 1978.

Ruland's collection of essays focuses on various aspects of Christmas with a general emphasis on pagan magico-cultic origins and Christian influences. Several foreign-language editions were published to help non-Germans understand German Christmas celebrations.

Russell, Ian. "A Survey of a Christmas Singing Tradition in South Yorkshire—1970." *Lore and Language*, 2 (1971-1975), 13-25.

Basically a survey of the distribution of a traditional singing event, this article does provide some historical and musicological analysis.

Ruth, Otto. *Der Lichterbaum. Germanischer Mythos und deutscher Volksbrauch*. Berlin: Abnenerbe, 1938.

Ruth is concerned with tree cults in Germanic mid-winter festivals, the tree's importance in religious cults of the Middle Ages, the status of trees in Germanic mythology, and their significance in the customs of Christmas.

Sabatini, P. *Le Costumanze del Natale*. Rome: Libreria Centrale, 1880.

Saer, Roy D. "The Christmas Carol-Singing Tradition in the Tanad Valley." *Folk Life*, 7 (1969), 15-42.

Saer describes the *plygain*, a carol service in the Tanad Valley of Wales. The names and types of carols are discussed as well as the subject matter they address, the history of the tradition, and some information on singers' attitudes toward the carols.

Salij, Jacek. "Teologia Ludowego Bozego Narodzenia." *Znak*, 24 (1972), 1526-43.

This article presents a theological analysis of the folk religious aspects of Christmas.

Samson, William. *The Book of Christmas*. New York and Toronto: McGraw-Hill, 1968.

Samson has produced an excellent popular book with beautiful photographs. He discusses origins and the symbolic significance of the elements of the celebration with an emphasis on survivals theory. An interesting analysis of love-hate feelings about Christmas is presented; the feelings result from the holiday's representation of birth and death (of the sun). Samson also provides a unique explanation of why children are receivers of gifts: because of Christian opposition to their pagan role as gifts themselves in sacrifices.

————. *Les Noëls du monde*. Paris: B. Arthaud, 1970.

This is the French translation of Samson's *The Book of Christmas* (see above).

Samuelson, Sue. "Nativity Scenes: Description and Analysis." *Folklore and Mythology Studies*, 3 (1979), 3-17.

This article surveys the form and history of Nativity scenes in Italy, France, and among Pennsylvania's Moravian communities. The analysis focuses on the impact of society, psychological orientations, geography, and religion on the scenes.

Sandys, William. *Christmas Carols, Ancient and Modern*. London: Richard Beckley, 1833; rpt. Norwood, Pa.: Norwood, 1973.

Although this book is mainly a collection of texts, the introduction includes extensive historical and descriptive material on English Christmas customs.

————. *Christmastide: Its History, Festivals and Carols*. London: John Russell Smith, 1860.

Sandys devotes most of his attention to court Christmas customs, particularly the historical development of. Christmas in England, with some continental references. He includes a brief discussion of general origins and the effect of Puritanism. Details of mistletoe, wassail, mumming, greenery, and gift-giving customs are provided. Although mainly descriptive, this book is not just a collection and should be read by anyone studying Christmas as it is cited repeatedly by later authors.

Sauermann, Dietmar. "Zur Diffusion des Weihnachtsbaumes in Westfalen, Probleme und Vorüberlegungen." *Zeitschrift für Volkskunde*, 20 (1973).

The diffusion of the Christmas tree in Westphalia is the subject of this report.

Schmechel, Linda L. "The Relationship of Children's Belief in Santa Claus to Causal Reasoning and Fantasy Predispositions." Diss. University of Texas, Austin, 1975.

Schmechel compares children's attitudes about Santa with their responses to Singer's Imaginative Play Predisposition Interview. As the child grows in cognitive maturity, questioning of Santa's existence increases, yet strong belief persists in some children with mature reasoning. Several levels of development may coexist. The Santa fantasy is an adaptive, ego-serving function which allows the child to cope with reality in an increasingly complex manner.

Schmidt, Leopold. "Der hängende Christbaum, Aus der Arbeit am Atlas der Burgenländischen Volkskundes." *Österreichische Zeitschrift für Volkskunde*, n.s., 17 (1963), 213-42.

The history of several different forms of the Christmas tree in central Europe is discussed: a wreath-like garland, a tree hung upside-down, and the standing tree.

Schmiecher, P.M. "What Do You Want for Christmas? The Social-Historical Theme." *Christian Century*, 89 (1972), 1294-98.

Although heavily theological, this essay does attempt some social-historical analysis along the lines of Mircea Eliade's *The Sacred and the Profane*.

Schneider, Camille. *Der Weihnachtsbaum und seine Heimat das Elsass*. Dornach, Switzerland: Philosophisch-Anthroposophischer Verlag am Goetheanum, 1965.

This is yet another German history of Christmas and the Christmas tree.

Scroggs, William O. "Christmas and the Payroll: Economic Importance of the Festival." *Outlook* (New York), 153 (1929), 621.

Scroggs points out the diverse industries which profit from the increased economic importance of Christmas: toy manufacturers, publishers and booksellers, the federal government (stamps, packages, import duties). He notes

the "recent" (the article was published in 1929) trend
toward more practical gifts as opposed to the turn-of-the-
century emphasis on gifts that lacked utility.

Scudder, Vida D. *Social Teachings of the Christian Year*.
New York: E.P. Dutton and Co., 1921.

This is an interpretation of Christmas from a heavily
theological point of view.

Seelatsie, Julie. "Christmas Among the Yakima." *Weewish
Tree*, 2, no. 3 (November, 1973), 6-7.

The Yakima Indians celebrate Christmas by dancing and
feasting.

Segal, Abraham. "Christmas in the Public Schools--The Problem." *Reconstructionist*, 14, no. 16 (10 December 1948),
17-22.

Segal looks at public school observances of Christian and
Jewish holidays as cultural, not religious, events. Christmas and Hanukkah, for example, mark the winter season; they
are human reactions to human problems.

Seidenspinner, Clarence, and Henry Schuman. *Great Protestant
Festivals*. New York: H. Wolff, 1952.

The authors present an interesting discussion of Church
Christmas pageants, decorations, and services.

Sereno, Renzo. "Some Observations on the Santa Claus Custom."
Psychiatry, 14 (1951), 387-96.

Sereno's pessimistic article discusses the deception of
children by adults via Santa Claus as a device to control
them. The question of control is also seen in the lack of
restraint at office Christmas parties. Christmas and Santa
Claus epitomize a flight from religion. The social customs
apparent at this time of year are an extrapolation of man's
inner problems.

Shlien, John. "Santa Claus: The Myth in America." *Human
Development Bulletin*, 6 (Spring, 1953), 27-32.

Santa Claus is a genuine "folk hero" since the story of
St. Nicholas/Santa Claus follows established patterns for
heroes' narratives. His yearly disappearance and recurrence
is equivalent to death and resurrection. He follows the
theme of the mysterious stranger. Santa functions as an
integrator of a diversified society, and the Santa custom's

effects on Jews and Blacks is explored, as is the manifestation of belief in children.

————. "Santa Claus: The Myth in America." *Etc., A Review of General Semantics*, 16 (1959), 389-400.

This essay is an expanded version of Shlien's earlier exploration of the topic (see above). The author is a psychotherapist who considers Santa Claus a "folk hero" who conforms to Lord Raglan's hero pattern. Santa's disappearance and recurrence is symbolic of death and resurrection, and there are further connections to Christ in Santa's role as a mysterious stranger. Santa creates social cohesion as an integrator of a diverse society since Christmas is the major holy day of the dominant white Anglo-Saxon society, which also includes Jews and Blacks. The children's attitude toward the Christmas celebration and its myths is a way of making moral and religious concepts understandable. It is also a way for elders to "mask their worship of what is ultimately sacred to them, love and responsibility to children who represent the future."

Shoemaker, A.L. *Christmas in Pennsylvania: A Folk-Cultural Study.* Kutztown, Pa.: Pennsylvania Folklore Society, 1959.

This book is mainly a descriptive work but Shoemaker does investigate the process of assimilation that many immigrant contributions underwent and the way in which Christmas fared in the acculturation process. The discussion of the development of Christmas trees and gift-bringers is especially good, but Shoemaker's analysis of the practice of "barring out the schoolmaster" makes no reference to similar role reversals that have existed since Roman times. He provides the only extensive material available on cookie cutters and Christmas cookies. The book relies heavily on newspaper accounts for documentation.

Shurmer, Pamela. "The Gift Game." *New Society*, 18 (1971), 1242-44.

Shurmer discusses gift exchange (particularly of Christmas gifts) in terms of how the importance of the relationship between sender and receiver is reflected in the value of a gift. She also notes how an initial gift begins a chain of reciprocity and how rejection can be adjusted through the gift's value. There is a statistical breakdown of the kinds of gifts given, such as gifts of luxury versus utility (and within utility, personal versus household) and who sends what kind of gift to whom. Egalitarian and

subordinate gift exchange is explored, and some thoughts
are presented on women's greater involvement in choosing
gifts as a representation of their overall importance in
conducting social relationships.

Skriver, Carl Anders. *Der Weihnachtsbaum, Geschichte und
      Sinndeutung.* Munich: Starczewski, 1966.

      Skriver presents a history of Christmas, the Christmas
      tree, and a discussion of Christmas symbolism.

Sloane, Valerie. "Debbie Shapiro and Santa Claus." *PTA
      Magazine*, 68, no. 4 (December, 1973), 22-25.

      Sloane advises Jewish parents on how to deal with Christ-
      mas and Hanukkah. What is important is not the exact
      resolution, but that the parents feel comfortable with it,
      and if they choose to celebrate just Hanukkah, that they
      firmly but kindly hold to their decision.

Smidt, J.R.H. de. *Les Noëls et la tradition populaire.*
      Diss. University of Groningue, 1932.

Smith, Peg. "Cornered at Christmas." *Transactional Analysis
      Journal*, 8 (1978), 326-27.

      Smith suggests some exercises and a reorientation of
      attitudes that people can use to better cope with the
      anxieties of Christmas.

Smith, Robert Jerome. "Social Folk Custom: Festivals and
      Celebrations." In *Folklore and Folklife*, ed. Richard
      Dorson. Chicago: University of Chicago Press, 1972.

      Smith's essay is a general work on the theory of fes-
      tivals, but has important applications to Christmas. One
      particular reference is to Christmas Club bank accounts
      which illustrate part of the economic function of festivals
      as a means of redistributing wealth.

Snyder, P.V. *The Christmas Tree Book: History of the Christ-
      mas Tree and Antique Christmas Tree Ornaments.* New York:
      Viking, 1977.

Sowers, Betty. "Christmas Customs from the Germans." *North
      Carolina Folklore*, 20 (1972), 171-73.

      Sowers's article is only a brief historical survey.

Spamer, Adolf. *Weihnachten in Alter und Neuer Zeit.* Jena: Eugen Diederichs, 1937.

Spamer's work is a typical historical/descriptive study of Christmas past and present. Sprinkled with wonderful photographs and illustrations are discussions of Nativity scenes, trees, St. Nicholas/Knecht Rupert/*Weihnachtsmann*, establishment of date and relationship to pagan death and sun festivals and customs.

Spencer, I.D. "Christmas, the Upstart." *New England Quarterly*, 8 (1935), 498-517.

Spencer focuses on the historical development of Christmas in New England as it progressed from Puritan repression to universal celebration.

Spencer, O.M. "Christmas Throughout Christendom." *Harper's*, 46 (1877), 241-57.

Although some historical material is presented, mostly on pagan contributions to Christmas customs, this article is mainly a descriptive survey.

Spicer, Dorothy Gladys. *The Book of Festivals.* New York: The Woman's Press, 1937.

Although basically descriptive, Spicer's book does provide an extensive Christmas bibliography.

————. "Christmas-tide Customs of the Syrian Immigrant." *Adult Bible Class Magazine*, 27 (December, 1932), 67-70.

Spicer's article, which is mainly descriptive, is the only work located pertaining to Christmas in Syria.

————. *Festivals of Western Europe.* New York: H.W. Wilson, 1958.

Like Spicer's other works, this book is descriptive. The bibliography is excellent.

Stenzel, J. "Western Christmas—in a Japanese Sense." *Christian Century*, 92 (1975), 1183-85.

Stenzel examines the reasons behind the Japanese adoption of Christmas. Some of the motivations are: imitation of the Americans during the occupation; the need for color and gaiety after the war; and providing an excuse to drink. The celebration has been changing with growing affluence and self-esteem, and with higher standards of living the

holiday has more of a home emphasis. The Japanese have
taken what they wanted from Christmas—its basic form—
discarded what was not needed—the deeper substance—and
added their own meanings.

Sterba, Richard. "A Dutch Celebration of a Festival."
    American Imago, 2 (1941), 205-8.

    Sterba notes the proximity of the Feast of the Innocents
and St. Stephen's Day to Christmas; they anticipate the
sacrificial death of Christ. Death symbolism is found in
Dutch children's play at being father and mother and doing
away with the parent of the same sex as the child. Christ
also rebelled against authority figures. Sterba also notes
parallels between the story of the Holy Family and Oedipus.

————. "On Christmas." *Psychoanalytic Quarterly*, 13 (1944),
    79-83.

    The emotional experiences at Christmas are an outgrowth
of its religious and archaic content. Parental behavior is
an acting out of childbirth. The period of excitement and
secret preparation before Christmas is akin to pregnancy;
the last-minute Christmas rush is labor; Christmas Day is
birth with its attendant exhaustion. People visit and
admire presents, which is equivalent to admiring a baby.
The fireplace and chimney associated with Santa are the
birth canal.

Stiller, Klaus. *Weihnachten*. Munich: Hanser, 1980.

Sweet, William. "Christmas in American History." *Chicago
    Theological Seminary Register*, 22 (November, 1932), 12-
    14.

    Sweet presents a brief survey of the European Christmas
celebration. His remarks on American Christmas are brief
and directed mainly toward the Puritan repression of the
holiday in the colonial era.

Taboada, Chivute. "Jesus, la Navidad gallego y sun ritual."
    Actas do Congresso Internationale de Ethnographie (Santo
    Tuso, 10-18 July 1963), 3 (1965), 569-94.

Thibaut, J.-B. "La Solennité de Noël." *Echos d'Orient*, 19
    (1920), 153-62.

    Thibaut discusses origins, the establishment of the date
of Christmas, its association with the Mithraic celebration

of Natalis Invicti, and the Eastern Church's observances
with their close association with Epiphany.

Thomas, Wilhelm, and Komrad Ameln. *Der Quempas Geht um,
Vergangheit und Zukunft eines deutschen Christnacht-
brauches.* Kassel: Bärenreiter, 1965.

This work is concerned with the origin and dissemination
of the Christmas tradition of singing *Quem pastores lauda-
vere.*

Ticktin, Harold. "A Jew Looks at Christmas." *US Catholic*,
38 (December, 1973), 24-28.

In this well-written and insightful article Ticktin
discusses Jews' feelings of discomfort at Christmas and
how Hanukkah seems second-rate to a Jewish child. He feels
Jewish holidays are more concerned with rules, as opposed
to the Christian emphasis on spirits or attitudes. There
is also a classic versus Romantic opposition as manifested
in Yom Kippur and Christmas, respectively.

Tiddy, R.J.E. *The Mummers' Play.* Oxford: Oxford University
Press, 1928.

Tiddy's main interest in mumming is as a survival from
pre-Christian and medieval times.

Tille, Alexander. "German Christmas and the Christmas Tree."
Folk-Lore, 3 (1892), 166-82.

Tille presents an overview of the history of the Christmas tree.

————. *Yule and Christmas, Their Place in the Germanic
Year.* London: David Nutt, 1899.

The author refutes earlier theories that Germanic tribes
were driven to a day of rest during the winter solstice.
Tille believes that the winter solstice is too hard to
actually observe and is of little economic importance.
Instead, he proposes that the Germanic peoples received
their winter holiday customs when they adopted the Roman
calendar. He believes that gift-giving arose from the
practice of giving children presents when a sibling (in
this case, Jesus) was born. The Christmas tree is the
union of the Roman custom of decorating the house with
greenery and the tenth-century legend that trees blossomed
and bore fruit at Christ's birth. The book contains a very
good discussion of the Church's relationship to secular

customs, its banning of them, gradual acceptance, and then repeated attempts to control them (which were unsuccessful). Tille discusses pre-Christian Yule (Jol/Jul) customs in Scandinavia and the effect of Roman observances, which were transmitted through the Catholic Church.

Tschude, Marie von. "Sentiment and Symbolisms Associated with Christmas." *House and Garden*, 15, no. 1 (January, 1909), 17-18.

This very simple article explores the pagan and Christian history of Christmas, especially the symbolism of greenery.

Tucker, Esther Jacobson. "The December Dilemma." *Reconstructionist*, 37, no. 9 (17 December 1971), 16-20.

Tucker provides good illustrations of the interface between Christmas and Hanukkah but advocates "beefing up" Hanukkah rather than have Christmas customs creep into its celebrations. Christmas is too powerful to ignore, so adjustments have to be made.

Tultseva, L.A. "Kalendarnye Religioznye Prazdniki v Bytu Sovremennogo Krestyanstva" ("Seasonal Religious Holidays in the Life of Today's Peasantry"). *Sovetskaya Etnografija*, 45, no. 6 (1970), 11-18.

Principal seasonal holidays are still observed in rural Russia but have lost their religious significance. At Christmas the religious feasting tradition is gone and what remains is just the merry-making aspect.

Usener, Hermann Karl. *Religiongeschichtliche Untersuchungen. Erster Teil: Das Weihnachtsfest*. Bonn: M. Cohen, 1889.

Usener's extensive examination of the history of Christmas emphasizes ecclesiastical history and the influences from the East, Rome, Egypt, and Mithraism.

Veiga de Oliveira, Ernesto. "A palha do Natal no Concelho de Vila do Conde." *Trabalhos de Antropologia e Etnologia*, 15 (1954), 107-10.

This brief article deals with the connection between Christmas and cults of the dead.

Violant i Simorra, Ramon. *El llibre de Nadal. Costums, creences, significat i origens*. Barcelona: Litografia Ramírez Cromoherma i Imprenta Salvador Salvadó, 1948.

Vloberg, Maurice. *Les Noëls de France.* Grenoble: B. Arthaud, 1934.

Vloberg's book is basically an historical survey of the Christmas festival. Emphasis is placed on the various days of the season, liturgical drama, mystery plays, pastorals, puppet theater, tales, songs, customs, and Nativity scenes.

Vogt, Evon Z. *Tortillas for the Gods: A Symbolic Analysis of Zinacanteco Rituals.* Cambridge, Mass.: Harvard University Press, 1976.

Vogt describes several Christmas rituals and analyzes them in terms of their connections with social relationships and non-Christian beliefs.

Waits, William Burnell, Jr. "The Many-Faced Custom: Christmas Gift-Giving in America, 1900-1940." Diss. Rutgers, 1978.

Gift exchanges in several different groups are discussed; the groups are distinguished by age, social relationship, sex, socioeconomic class, and employment. Patterns vary from group to group, but many present-day aspects of gift-giving became rationalized between 1900 and 1940, such as choosing practical gifts for men and luxurious ones for women. The research is based on general periodical and trade journal accounts centering on the white Protestant middle class.

Wallach, Michael A., and Margaret I. Leggett. "Testing the Hypothesis That a Person Will Be Consistent: Stylistic Consistency vs. Situation Specificity in the Size of Children's Drawings." *Journal of Personality,* 40 (1972), 309-30.

The size of children's drawings of Santa Claus becomes larger as Christmas approaches.

Wallis, Wilson D. *Culture and Progress.* New York: McGraw-Hill, 1930.

In a chapter on the assimilation of culture traits, Wallis explores the history and diffusion of some Christmas customs: trees, cards, and mistletoe. He makes some brief comments on the spread of Christmas customs to Moslem Turkish families in Istanbul. The customs are adopted for the sake of the children, who have observed neighboring Christian families' celebrations. The situation is also

due to the influence of other Western traits in Moslem life.
The parallel with Jewish problems with Christmas is intriguing.

Walser, Richard. "His Worship, the John Kerner." *North
    Carolina Folklore*, 19 (1971), 160-72.

Walser has produced a mainly descriptive work about the
Junkanoo festival as it was observed among North Carolina
antebellum slaves.

Walsh, William. *The Story of Santa Klaus*. New York: Moffat,
    Yard, 1909; rpt. Detroit: Gale, 1970.

This historical/descriptive analysis of Santa Claus and
other gift bringers also provides a history of pagan celebrations, the Christmas tree, the Magi, Twelfth Night customs,
and pantomimes.

Walwin, Peggy C. *St. Nicholas, Our Santa Claus*. Gloucester,
    Mass.: Albert E. Smith, 1971.

The book focuses on the history and iconography of St.
Nicholas, his relation to Santa Claus, and various churches,
hospitals, schools, and geographical designations bearing
the name of St. Nicholas.

Warner, W. Lloyd. *The Family of God: A Symbolic Study of
    Christian Life in America*. New Haven: Yale University
    Press, 1961.

Warner makes scattered references to Christmas throughout
his book, particularly noting the rise in emotions from
Advent to Christmas Day and the secularization of the
Virgin Mary's role at Christmas. He also points out how,
despite the diversity of American experience, common feelings
are expressed symbolically in the emphasis on the family at
Christmastime (and at Mother's Day and Thanksgiving).

Warren, Nathan Boughton. *Christmas in the Olden Time, Its
    Customs and Their Origin*. London: James Pattie and
    George Glaisher, 1859; rpt. Folcroft, Pa.: Folcroft
    Library Editions, 1976.

Warren describes "ancient" Christmas customs and their
origins, such as the practice of barring the door or making
provision for the poor. He gives some historical material
on the influence of Druids and Mithraism, accompanied by
valuable comments on Christmas foods.

————. *The Holidays, Christmas, Easter, and Whitsuntide, Their Social Festivities, Customs, and Carols.* New York: Hurd and Houghton, 1868.

Warren alleges that the first religious observances of Christmas were held in A.D. 98. He points out that the invention of printing contributed to a decrease in pageants and other religious shows because books were a better means of popular instruction. The mysteries of Christmas degenerated into burlesques, masques, or mummeries. Carols were introduced into England by Italian clergymen to replace heathen Yule/wassail songs.

Waterman, A.T. *A Lecture on the Christmas Festival*, 2nd ed. Providence, R.I.: Wilcox and Co., 1835.

Weber, Wilhelmine. "Winter Festivals of Mexico: A Christmas That Combines Aztec and Christian Legends." *Craftsman*, 23 (1912), 266-74.

Christmas in Mexico is a combination of the "religious fanatic and joyous pagan." It centers around the Virgin and combines Spanish and Aztec elements.

Weber-Kellermann, Ingeborg. "Exkurs: Die deutsche Burgerfamilie und ihre Weihnachtslichen Verhaltenmuster." In her *Die deutsche Familie, Versuch einer Sozialgeschichte*, 2nd ed. Frankfurt: Insel, 1976, pp. 300-11.

The author surveys the history of Christmas, especially in the context of German middle-class society over the last several centuries. She stresses that while Christmas changes, it does so because people need to make it fit their needs. However, it will always symbolize human hopes and dreams and mark a point in the cycle of the year in which people are free to feel playful and happy.

————. "Herrscheklas und Herrschedame, Zwei Brauchgestalten der Weihnachtszeit aus dem Thüringer Wald und ihre Geschichte." *Deutsches Jahrbuch für Volkskunde*, 6 (1960), 91-104.

The author explores the history of the Christmas giftgiver, *Herrschedame*, and associated figures such as St. Nicholas, St. Thomas, and the Christ-Child. She places special emphasis on the influence of Luther on the figures and on Christmas in general.

————. *Das Weihnachtsfest, Eine Kultur- und Sozialgeschichte der Weihnachtszeit.* Luzern and Frankfurt/M: C.J. Bucher, 1978.

Weber-Kellermann's book is a collection of her studies of various aspects of family-oriented Christmas celebrations, such as trees, gifts, gift-givers, and toys, with supplementary chapters on Advent, New Year's, and Epiphany.

Weightman, Gavin. "Role of Christmas." *New Society*, 38 (1976), 633.

This is a very good discussion of the various manifestations of role-reversal behavior during Christmas. Reversal practices are dying out, perhaps because Christmas is now celebrated more in the home. The best example is at the office Christmas party, but the guilt that usually follows such occasions illustrates the conflict between the party's revelry and feelings of general irreverence and the burden of family responsibility. Weightman notes that role reversals are no longer common in the hierarchical organizations where one would expect to find them, such as the military. Nowadays, the principal role reversal is spending money on gifts, cards, decorations, charities, etc., as a part of the season's essence and as a levelling of social distinctions. Weightman also notes that role reversal takes place during a period when "normal" or "profane" time is suspended.

Weiser, F.X. *Christmas Book.* New York: Harcourt, Brace, 1952.

Although geared to a popular audience, Weiser's work nonetheless provides good information on a variety of Christmas customs: cards, Nativity scenes and plays, trees, plants and flowers, food, St. Nicholas and Santa Claus, and gift exchange. There is some material on the general history of Christmas, a good topic index, and some reference notes.

————. *Handbook of Christmas Customs.* New York: Harcourt, 1958.

Weiser's book is a good survey of the historical development of Christmas customs involving the entire season from Advent to Epiphany. He comments on the liturgical elements as well as the popular Christmas customs. He also includes some linguistic material.

Weiser-Aall, Lily. "Julenissen og julegeita i Norge." *Små-skrifter fra Norsk Etnologisk Gransking*, 4 (1954), 1-91.

This is a folkloristic comparative survey of Christmas elves, spirits, and gift-bringers in Norway. It also contains some material on cards and masks.

————. "Juletreet i Norge." *Norveg*, 2 (1952), 21-84.

This work is concerned with the history of the Christmas tree in Norway.

Wernecke, Herbert. *Celebrating Christmas Around the World*. Philadelphia: Westminster Press, 1962.

This is a collection of essays on Christmas customs and reactions from around the world, including places with little other Christmas literature: the Congo, Palestine, Armenia, Iraq, Micronesia, Iran, and Thailand. Europe and North and South America are also given their due. There is some very interesting material on Christmas at West Point and Annapolis.

————. *Christmas Songs and Their Stories*. Philadelphia: Westminster Press, 1957.

Wernecke gives the texts and brief histories of fifty-four Christmas carols.

Westcott, Joan. "Witchcraft and Yuletide." *New Society*, 4, no. 117 (24 December 1964), 5-6.

This is mainly a descriptive article that really has little to do with Christmas.

Whistler, Laurence. *The English Festivals*. London: William Heinemann Ltd., 1947.

Whistler's description and history of Christmas concentrates on the tree, presents, Father Christmas, the influence of Dickens, carols, lights, cards, greenery, the Yule log, and food.

————. *The Kissing Bough, a Christmas Custom*. London: William Heinemann Ltd., 1953.

Whistler manages to present some symbolic analysis in this mainly descriptive work devoted to a cousin of the mistletoe Christmas custom.

Whitaker-Wilson, C. "History of Three Great Festivals."
  Fortnightly Review, 129 (January, 1928), 34-37.

  The author discusses the establishment of the date of
  celebration of the Nativity, and the history of Santa Claus,
  kissing under the mistletoe, and the wassail bowl.

Wilson, R.C. "How Christmas Came to America." *American
  Forests*, 67 (December, 1961), 8-9, 50-52.

  Wilson presents a simple, general survey of the development of Christmas customs in America, paying particular
  attention to the effects of the waves of immigrants in
  the 1800s.

Wirth, Àlfred. "Alte Weihnachtsbräuche in Anhalt und ihre
  Deutung." *Dessauer Kulturspiegel*, 3 (1956), 416-21.

  This is another standard article on the origins of old
  Christmas customs.

Witt, Louise. "The Jew Celebrates Christmas." *Christian
  Century*, 56 (1939), 1497-99.

  The Jew of the 1930s observed Christmas more than before.
  He participated in the spirit, not the theology, of the
  holiday. Witt feels that the Jews' participation could
  decrease hostility toward them and stresses the importance
  of the lure of the dominant culture. (See Leonard Gross's
  article above for a 1965 viewpoint.)

Wolf, Eric. "Santa Claus: Notes on a Collective Representation." In *Process and Pattern in Culture: Essays in
  Honor of Julian H. Steward*. Chicago: Aldine, 1964, pp.
  147-55.

  Wolf surveys the development of the Santa Claus figure.
  It began in Europe but is mainly a "self-conscious creation
  of individuals engaged in creating a new American culture."
  He credits the influence of Pintard, Irving, Moore, and
  Nast. Santa Claus is a very important mythical figure in
  a highly secularized society. He is a part of a larger
  idealistic complex relating adults to children. His economic
  aspects involve goods and power and financial success.
  Santa is a grandfatherly type, a guardian of morality which
  is really the morality of the marketplace; Santa Claus is
  the appropriate collective representation of commodity
  fetishism.

Yeager, Lyn Allison. "The Flowers of Christmas." *Tennessee Folklore Society Bulletin*, 39 (1973), 113-18.

Yeager gives a history of various kinds of Christmas plants: holly, ivy, mistletoe, poinsettia, tree, Glastonbury thorn, herbs, and bayberry, among others.

Young, Chester Raymond. "The Observance of Old Christmas in Southern Appalachia." *Appalachian Journal*, 4 (1977), 147-58.

The customs and beliefs associated with Christmas in Appalachia are the result of resistance to changes in the calendar which occurred in 1753.

Zawistowicz, Kazimiera. "Obrzędowość Swiąt Bożego Narodzenia" ("The Ritual of Christmas"). *Wiedza i Zyrie*, 8 (1933), 956-66.

SUBJECT INDEX

ADVENT: Fink; Kellner; Weber-Kellermann, *Das Weihnachtsfest*;
    Weiser, *Christmas Book*
AFRICA: Wernecke, *Celebrating* ...
ALSACE: Kronfeld
AMERICAN INDIANS: Baur; Burland; Colson; Faye; Léon-Portilla;
    Neuhoff; Seelatsie
ANTHROPOLOGICAL APPROACHES: Bricker; Jaakola; Koleva
APPALACHIA: Young
ARMENIA: Wernecke, *Celebrating* ...
ART: Berglund; Cesaresco; Ebon; Ghéon; Grigson; Kissling;
    Mak, *Middeleeuwse* ...; Muir; Müller; Onasch; Poulaille;
    Rietschel
ASTURIAS: Alvarez Solar-Quintes
AUSTRALIA: Anonymous, "Chrissy for the Surfer"; Cusack;
    Harrison
AUSTRIA: Harrison; Kronfeld
AZTEC: Weber
BELLS: Krythe, *All About Christmas*
BOAR'S HEAD: Hare; Ernest Jones
BOHEMIA: Anonymous, "Wien und der Weihnachtskrippenbau ...";
    Bencker; Jelinkova
BOLIVIA: Fortún
BOXING DAY (ST. STEPHEN'S DAY): Hadfield; Müller
BRAZIL: Lamas
BREADS: Höfler. (See also FOOD)
CAKE: Lid, *Joleband*. (See also FOOD)
CANADA: Brummer; Gordon Cox, both titles; Halpert
CANDLES: Chesterton, "The Yule Log ..."; Crooke; Ewert;
    Finckh
CARDS: Alemany Vich; Baker; Buday; Chase; Cowie; Dearborn;
    Ettlinger; Goodbar; J. Gross; Hadfield; Harrison; Hill;
    Hole, *British Folk Customs*; Sheila Johnson, both titles;
    Krythe, *All About Christmas*; Kunz; Lassen; Myers; Palmer;
    Petersen; Pimlott, *The Englishman's Christmas*; Riemer-
    schmidt; Ristow; Wallis; Weiser, *Christmas Book*, Weiser-
    Aall, "Julenissen ..."; Whistler, *The English Festivals*
CARIBBEAN: Abrahams, all titles; Dirks; Mennesson-Rigaud

CAROLLING: Gordon Cox, both titles; Crawford; Kapros; Russell;
     Saer
CAROLS AND SONGS: Anonymous, "Doggerel in the Manger"; Barnett,
     The American Christmas; Brooks; R.J. Campbell; Cesaresco;
     Coffin; Dearmer; Emurian; Fiedler; Gastoué; Gennep; Ghéon;
     Hoover; Koleva; Krumscheid; Mottinger; Müller; Myers;
     Nettel, both titles; Nettl; Palmer; Pearson; Petneki;
     Pimlott, "Arts in Society"; Poston; Poulaille; Riddlehough;
     Saer; Sandys, *Christmas Carols*; Thomas; Vloberg; Warren,
     The Holidays ...; Wernecke, *Christmas Songs* ...; Whistler,
     The English Festivals
CHILD, IMPORTANCE OF: Barnett, "Christmas ..."; Burns; R.J.
     Campbell; Isambert, *La Fin* ...; Proctor; Samson, both
     titles; Shlien; Sterba, "A Dutch Celebration ..."
CHILDERMAS: Hadfield
CHINA: Feilburg
CHRISTMAS SEALS/STAMPS: Krythe, *All About Christmas*; Lenz
CHURCH: See ECCLESIASTICAL APPROACH
COMMERCIALIZATION: Burland; Chesterton, "On Christmas ...,"
     "The Spirit of Christmas"; Harvey Cox; Hugh Duncan; Dundes;
     Foley; Jack; Parker; Roberts. (See also ECONOMICS)
COOKIES: Höfler; Shoemaker. (See also FOOD)
DATE OF CHRISTMAS, ESTABLISHING THE: Botte; R.J. Campbell;
     Duchesne; Frazer; Gastoué; Jekels; Ernest Jones; Kellner;
     Lake, "Christmas"; Meyer; Monks; Montero; Muir; Onasch;
     Spamer; Thibaut; Whitaker-Wilson
DEATH: Anonymous, "Christmas Customs and Their Origins";
     Anonymous, "Ritual and Meaning"; Evans; Feilburg; Gailey;
     Geiger; Lévi-Strauss, "What Does ..."; Robert Reid;
     Robert; Samson; Viega de Oliveira
DEPRESSION AT CHRISTMAS: Anonymous, "Christmas and Suicide";
     Battle; Catell; Gary Collins; Etzioni; Leiber; Marti-
     Ibeñez; Peg Smith
DICKENS: Barnett, *The American Christmas*; Coffin; Philip
     Collins; Curtis; Holderness; Nettel, *Christmas and Its
     Carols*; Pimlott, *The Englishman's Christmas*; Whistler,
     The English Festivals
DRAMA: Babb; Bencker; R.J. Campbell; Thomas Campbell; Carneiro;
     Cesaresco; Chambers; Gastoué; Köppen; Lamas; MacGregor-
     Villareal; Mannhardt; Margetson; Monks; Müller; Myers;
     Pearce; Pearson; Pimlott, *The Englishman's Christmas*;
     Poulaille; Riemerschmidt; Vloberg; Weiser, *Christmas Book*
ECCLESIASTICAL APPROACH: Anonymous, *El libro de Navidad*;
     Botte; Conybeare; Duchesne; Dunphy; Ellekilde, *Vor danske
     Jul*; Gaillard; Gastoué; Ghéon; Hartke; Kellner; Leclercq;
     McArthur; Meyer; Montero; Müller; Onasch; Pearson;
     Poulaille; Richards; Rodgers; Salij; Seidenspinner;

Thibaut; Thomas; Tille, *Yule and Christmas*; Usener; Weiser,
Handbook ...
ECONOMICS: Anonymous, "La Navidad ..."; Colson; J. Davis;
Susan G. Davis; Hugh Duncan; Dundes; Evans; Fri; Scroggs;
Robert Smith; Wolf. (See also COMMERCIALIZATION)
EGG NOG: Lenz
ELVES: Ellekilde, "Af julenissens historie"; Weiser-Aall,
"Julenissen ..."
ENGLAND: Holder; Huekin; Lebech; Pimlott, all titles; Whistler
EPIPHANY: Anonymous, "La Navidad ..."; Conybeare; Gennep;
Hadfield; Hartke; Kellner; McArthur; Mak, *Het Kerstfest*;
Marbach; Müller; Thibaut; Walsh; Weber-Kellermann, *Das
Weihnachtsfest*; Weiser, *Christmas Book*
FAMILY, IMPORTANCE OF: Barnett, both titles; Benney; Bossard;
Gennep; Isambert, *La Fin* ...; Lueschen, both titles;
Murdock; Ribeyrol; Warner; Weber-Kellerman, "Exkurs ..."
FEAST OF FOOLS: du Tilliot; Hadfield; James; Pimlott, "Merry
Christmas"
FERTILITY: Anonymous, "Christmas Customs and Their Origins";
Eskeröd, "Julhalmen ..."; Evans; Geiger; Lid, "Joles-
veiner ..."; Heather Miller
FINLAND: Jaakola
FIRE: Chesterton, "The Yule Log ..."; Gennep; Heather Miller
FLOWERS: Tille, *Yule and Christmas*; Weiser, *Christmas Book*;
Yeager. (See also GREENERY)
FOOD: Anonymous, "La Nochebuena ..."; Anonymous, "Zur Erkennt-
nis ..."; Ghéon; Hare; Höfler; Holder; Koleva; Krythe,
All About Christmas; Lid, *Joleband*; Montgomery; Myers;
Pearson; Pimlott, *The Englishman's Christmas*; Richard;
Riemerschmidt; Shoemaker; Warren, *Christmas* ...; Weiser,
Christmas Book; Whistler, *The English Festivals*
FRANCE: Bosch; Gennep; Isambert, both titles; Janvier;
Harrison; Nitzsche; Samuelson; Smidt; Vloberg
GERMANY: Anonymous, "Zur Erkenntnis ..."; Bencker; Botte;
Bülow; Cassel; Fehrle; Flusser; Harrison; Höfler; Koch;
Köppen; Kutter; Müller; Nitzsche; Riemerschmidt; Ruland;
Schmidt; Schneider; Sowers; Spamer; Tille, both titles;
Weber-Kellermann, all titles
GIFT-GIVERS: Berglund; Dorson; Ehrensvärd; Harrison; Kutter;
Lebech; Lévi-Strauss, both titles; Meyer; Palmer; Pimlott,
The Englishman's Christmas; Sandys, *Christmastide*; Shoe-
maker; Spamer; Walsh; Weber-Kellermann, "Herrscheklas ...,"
Das Weihnachtsfest; Weiser-Aall, "Julenissen ...";
Whistler, *The English Festivals*
GIFT-GIVING/EXCHANGE/GIFTS: Anonymous, "La Navidad ...";
Barnett, both titles; Beattie; Becker; Belfrage; Boyer;
J. Davis; Hadfield; Hole, *British Folk Custom*; Meerloo;
E.F. Miller; Moos; Moschetti; Pearson; Scroggs; Shurmer;

GIFT-GIVING/EXCHANGE/GIFTS (cont'd)
   Tille, *Yule and Christmas*; Waits; Walsh; Weber-Kellermann,
   Das Weihnachtsfest; Weiser, *Christmas Book*; Whistler, *The
   English Festivals*
GIFTS: See GIFT-GIVING
GLASTONBURY THORN: Yeager. (See also GREENERY)
GREENERY: F. Duncan; Hadfield; Hare; Hole, *British Folk Cus-
   toms*; Hyams; Krythe, *All About Christmas*; Lid, *Joleband* ...;
   Myers; Palmer; Pearson; Sandys, *Christmastide*; Tille, both
   titles; Tschude; Weiser, *Christmas Book*; Whistler, *The
   English Festivals*; Yeager. (See also FLOWERS; HOLLY;
   MISTLETOE; WREATH)
HANUKKAH: See JEWS AND CHRISTMAS
HISTORY (GENERAL): Anonymous, *El libro de Navidad*; Appia;
   Auld; Baker; Botte; Burland; R.J. Campbell; Thomas Camp-
   bell; Cassel; Chabot; Chambers; Coffin; Colditz; Count;
   Cowie; Crippen; Davenport-Adams; Dawson; Deems; Douglas;
   Fehrle; Feilburg; Frazer; Geiger; Ghéon; Grolman; Gwynne;
   Hadfield; Hare; Harrison; Hartke; Hervey; Hole, *Christ-
   mas* ...; Jack; James; Leslie Dent Johnson; Kemp; Krythe,
   both titles; Lake, both titles; Latey; Lenz; Lévi-Strauss,
   "Le Père Noël ..."; Lid, "Um Upphavet ..."; Liman;
   McArthur; McCurdy; Mak, *Het Kerstfest*; Mannhardt; Marbach;
   Meyer; Miles; Monks; Muir; Müller; Myers; Nilsson,
   "Studien ..."; Onasch; Palmer; Pearson; Pimlott, *The
   Englishman's Christmas*, "Merry Christmas"; Poulaille;
   Robert Reid; Richards; Ruland; Samson, both titles;
   Sandys, *Christmastide*; Schmiecher; Schneider; Skriver;
   Spamer; O.M. Spencer; Spicer, *The Book of Festivals*,
   Festivals ...; Stiller; Sweet; Taboada; Thibaut; Tille,
   Yule and Christmas; Tschude; Usener; Vloberg; Waits;
   Wallis; Warren; Waterman; Weiser, both titles; Westcott;
   Whistler, both titles; Wirth. (See also PAGAN CUSTOMS;
   individual countries)
HOLLAND: Sterba, "A Dutch Celebration ..."
HOLLY: Ingersoll; Yeager. (See also GREENERY)
HUNGARY: Bencker; Manga
IMMIGRANT GROUPS (in United States): Barnett, *The American
   Christmas*; Baur; Bock; Canter, both titles; Galanti;
   Charles W. Jones; Neuhoff; Wilson
INDIANS: See AMERICAN INDIANS
IRAN: Čaltić; Wernecke, *Celebrating* ...
IRAQ: Wernecke, *Celebrating* ...
IRELAND: Gailey; Glassie
ITALY: Botte; Harrison; Sabatini; Samuelson
JAPAN: Plath; Stenzel
JEWS AND CHRISTMAS: Canter, both titles; Clemente; Bea Fire-
   stone; Goldin; L. Gross; Harris; Hirsch; Lincoln; Maller;

94 Subject Index

NEW ENGLAND: Brown; I.D. Spencer
NEW YEAR'S: Bø; Ellekilde, *Vor danske Jul* ...; Hartke; Mak,
    Het Kerstfest; Marti-Ibeñez; Müller; Weber-Kellermann,
    Das Weihnachtsfest
NEW YORK: Charles W. Jones; Neuhoff
OFFICE PARTIES: See PARTIES
PAGAN CUSTOMS: Count; Dawson; F. Duncan; Feilburg; Frazer;
    Geiger; Grolman; Hare; Harrison; Hayden; Leslie Dent
    Johnson; Lid, "Jolesveiner ..."; McArthur; Mak, *Het
    Kerstfest*; Marbach; Meyer; Müller; Nettel, *Christmas and
    Its Carols*; Nilsson, "Studien ..."; Palmer; Reid; Ruland;
    Samson, both titles; Spamer; Tille, *Yule and Christmas*;
    Usener; Walsh; Warren. (See also HISTORY)
PARTIES: Colson; Holland
PENNSYLVANIA: Samuelson; Shoemaker. (See also PENNSYLVANIA-
    GERMANS)
PENNSYLVANIA-GERMANS: Fogel; Nitzsche; Shoemaker
PIONEERS: Baur
POINSETTIA: Yeager. (See also FLOWERS; GREENERY)
POLAND: Ginalska; Klinger; Pischel; Zawistowicz
PORTUGAL: Chaves
PRESENTS: See GIFT-GIVING
PSYCHOLOGICAL APPROACHES: Anonymous, "Christmas and Suicide";
    Anonymous, "Vision of Reality"; Barnett, both titles;
    Battle; Benjamin; Berne; Boyer; Bryant; Cole; Gary Collins;
    Coyle; Eisenbud; Eskeröd, *Årets Åring*; Etzioni; Fehr;
    Galdston; Groöt, both titles; Jekels; Ernest Jones; Leiber;
    Levy; Marti-Ibeñez; Prentice; Proctor; Robert Reid;
    Roodin; Samuelson; Sereno; Peg Smith; Sterba, both titles
PUBLIC SCHOOLS: See SCHOOLS, CHRISTMAS IN THE
PURITANS, INFLUENCE OF: Brown; Curtis; Fiedler; Hare; Myers;
    Nettel, *Christmas and Its Carols*; Neuhoff; Palmer; Pearson;
    Pigot; Pimlott, "Merry Christmas," *The Englishman's Christ-
    mas*; Sandys, *Christmastide*; I.D. Spencer; Sweet
PYRAMID: Fritzsch; Lauffer. (See also NATIVITY SCENES)
REBIRTH OF THE SUN: Maleš; Marti-Ibeñez; Heather Miller
ROMANIA: Alexe
RUDOLPH THE RED-NOSED REINDEER: Barnett, *The American Christmas*;
    Dundes
RUSSIA: Agursij; Koleva; Nosova; Tultseva
ST. BARBARA'S DAY: Müller
ST. NICHOLAS: Bock; Chambers; Ebon; Gilst; Groöt, both titles;
    McKnight; Meerloo; Müller; Oswalt; Redl; Riemerschmidt;
    Walwin; Weiser, *Christmas Book*
ST. STEPHEN'S DAY: See BOXING DAY
ST. THOMAS'S DAY: Müller